Vanita

Polite Stories

Vernon Lee

Alpha Editions

This edition published in 2024

ISBN : 9789362928566

Design and Setting By
Alpha Editions
www.alphaedis.com
Email - info@alphaedis.com

Contents

LADY TAL.

The church of the Salute, with its cupolas and volutes, stared in at the long windows, white, luminous, spectral. A white carpet of moonlight stretched to where they were sitting, with only one lamp lit, for fear of mosquitoes. All the remoter parts of the vast drawing-room were deep in gloom; you were somehow conscious of the paintings and stuccos of the walls and vaulted ceilings without seeing them. From the canal rose plash of oar, gondolier's cry, and distant guitar twang and quaver of song; and from the balconies came a murmur of voices and women's laughter. The heavy scent of some flower, vague, white, southern, mingled with the cigarette smoke in that hot evening air, which seemed, by contrast to the Venetian day, almost cool.

As Jervase Marion lolled back (that lolling of his always struck one as out of keeping with his well-adjusted speech, his precise mind, the something conventional about him) on the ottoman in the shadow, he was conscious of a queer feeling, as if, instead of having arrived from London only two hours ago, he had never ceased to be here at Venice, and under Miss Vanderwerf's hospitable stuccoed roof. All those years of work, of success, of experience (or was it not rather of study?) of others, bringing with them a certain heaviness, baldness, and scepticism, had become almost a dream, and this present moment and the similar moment twelve years ago remaining as the only reality. Except his hostess, whose round, unchangeable face, the face of a world-wise, kind but somewhat frivolous baby, was lit up faintly by the regular puffs of her cigarette, all the people in the room were strangers to Marion: yet he knew them so well, he had known them so long.

There was the old peeress, her head tied up in a white pocket-handkerchief, and lolling from side to side with narcoticised benevolence, who, as it was getting on towards other people's bedtime, was gradually beginning to wake up from the day's slumber, and to murmur eighteenth-century witticisms and Blessingtonian anecdotes. There was the American Senator, seated with postage-stamp profile and the attitude of a bronze statesman, against the moonlight, one hand in his waistcoat, the other incessantly raised to his ear as in a stately "Beg pardon?" There was the depressed Venetian naval officer who always made the little joke about not being ill when offered tea; the Roumanian Princess who cultivated the reputation of saying spiteful things cleverly, and wore all her pearls for fear of their tarnishing; the English cosmopolitan who was one day on the Bosphorus and the next in Bond Street, and was wise about singing and acting; the well turned out, subdued, Parisian-American æsthete talking with an English accent about modern pictures and ladies' dresses; and the awkward, enthusiastic English æsthete, who considered Ruskin a ranter and creaked over the marble floors with dusty, seven-mile boots. There was a solitary spinster fresh from higher efforts of some sort, unconscious that no one in Venice appreciated her classic profile, and that everyone in Venice stared at her mediæval dress and collar of coins from the British Museum. There was the usual bevy of tight-waisted Anglo-Italian girls ready to play the guitar and sing, and the usual supply of shy, young artists from the three-franc pensions, wandering round the room, candle in hand, with the niece of the house, looking with shy intentness at every picture and sketch and bronze statuette and china bowl and lacquer box.

The smoke of the cigarettes mingled with the heavy scent of the flowers; the plash of oar and snatch of song rose from the canal; the murmur and laughter entered from the balcony. The old peeress lolled out her Blessingtonian anecdotes; the Senator raised his hand to his ear and said "Beg pardon?" the Roumanian Princess laughed shrilly at her own malignant sayings; the hostess's face was periodically illumined by her cigarette and the hostess's voice periodically burst into a childlike: "Why, you don't mean it!" The young men and women flirted in undertones about Symonds, Whistler, Tolstoy, and the way of rowing gondolas, with an occasional chord struck on the piano, an occasional string twanged on the guitar. The Salute, with its cupolas and volutes, loomed spectral in at the windows; the moonlight spread in a soft, shining carpet to their feet.

Jervase Marion knew it all so well, so well, this half-fashionable, half-artistic Anglo-American idleness of Venice, with its poetic setting and its prosaic reality. He would have known it, he felt, intimately, even if he had never seen it before; known it so as to be able to make each of these people say in print what they did really say. There is something in being a psychological novelist, and something in being a cosmopolitan American, something in being an inmate of the world of Henry James and a kind of Henry James, of a lesser magnitude, yourself: one has the pleasure of understanding so much, one loses the pleasure of misunderstanding so much more.

A singing boat came under the windows of Palazzo Bragadin, and as much of the company as could, squeezed on to the cushioned gothic balconies, much to the annoyance of such as were flirting outside, and to the satisfaction of such as were flirting within. Marion—who, much to poor Miss Vanderwerf's disgust, had asked to be introduced to no one as yet, but to be allowed to realise that evening, as he daintily put it, that Venice was the same and he a good bit changed—Marion leaned upon the parapet of a comparatively empty balcony and looked down at the canal. The moonbeams were weaving a strange, intricate pattern, like some old Persian tissue, in the dark water; further off the yellow and red lanterns of the singing boat were surrounded by black gondolas, each with its crimson, unsteady prow-light; and beyond, mysterious in the moonlight, rose the tower and cupola of St. George, the rigging of ships, and stretched a shimmering band of lagoon.

He had come to give himself a complete holiday here, after the grind of furnishing a three-volume novel for Blackwood (Why did he write so much? he asked himself; he had enough of his own, and to spare, for a dainty but frugal bachelor); and already vague notions of new stories began to arrive in his mind. He determined to make a note of them and dismiss them for the time. He had determined to be idle; and he was a very methodical man, valuing above everything (even above his consciousness of being a man of the world) his steady health, steady, slightly depressed spirits, and steady, monotonous, but not unmanly nor unenjoyable routine of existence.

Jervase Marion was thinking of this, and the necessity of giving himself a complete rest, not letting himself be dragged off into new studies of mankind and womankind; and listening, at the same time, half-unconsciously, to the scraps of conversation which came from the other little balconies, where a lot of heads were grouped, dark in the moonlight.

"I do hope it will turn out well—at least not too utterly awful," said the languid voice of a young English manufacturer's heir, reported to live exclusively off bread and butter and sardines, and to have no further desires in the world save those of the amiable people who condescended to shoot on his moors, yacht in his yachts, and generally devour his millions, "it's ever so long since I've been wanting a sideboard. It's rather hard lines for a poor fellow to be unable to find a sideboard ready made, isn't it? And I have my doubts about it even now."

There was a faint sarcastic tinge in the languid voice; the eater of bread and butter occasionally felt vague amusement at his own ineptness.

"Nonsense, my dear boy," answered the cosmopolitan, who knew all about acting and singing; "it's sure to be beautiful. Only you must *not* let them put on that rococo cornice, quite out of character, my dear boy."

"A real rococo cornice is a precious lot better, I guess, than a beastly imitation Renaissance frieze cut with an oyster knife," put in a gruff New York voice. "That's my view, leastways."

"I think Mr. Clarence had best have it made in slices, and each of you gentlemen design him a slice—that's what's called original nowadays—*c'est notre façon d'entendre l'art aujourd'hui*," said the Roumanian Princess.

A little feeble laugh proceeded from Mr. Clarence. "Oh," he said, "I shouldn't mind that at all. I'm not afraid of my friends. I'm afraid of myself, of my fickleness and weak-mindedness. At this rate I shall never have a sideboard at all, I fear."

"There's a very good one, with three drawers and knobs, and a ticket 'garantito vero noce a lire 45,' in a joiner's shop at San Vio, which I pass every morning. You'd much better have that, Mr. Clarence. And it would be a new departure in art and taste, you know."

The voice was a woman's; a little masculine, and the more so for a certain falsetto pitch. It struck Marion by its resolution, a sort of highbred bullying and a little hardness about it.

"Come, don't be cruel to poor Clarence, Tal darling," cried Miss Vanderwerf, with her kind, infantine laugh.

"Why, what have I been saying, my dear thing?" asked the voice, with mock humility; "I only want to help the poor man in his difficulties."

"By the way, Lady Tal, will you allow me to take you to Rietti's one day?" added an æsthetic young American, with a shadowy Boston accent; "he has some things you ought really to see, some quite good tapestries, a capital Gubbio vase. And he has a carved nigger really by Brustolon, which you ought to get for your red room at Rome. He'd look superb. The head's restored and one of the legs, so Rietti'd let him go for very little. He really is an awfully jolly bit of carving—and in that red room of yours——;"

"Thanks, Julian. I don't think I seem to care much about him. The fact is, I have to see such a lot of ugly white men in my drawing-room, I feel I really couldn't stand an ugly black one into the bargain."

Here Miss Vanderwerf, despite her solemn promise, insisted on introducing Jervase Marion to a lady of high literary tastes, who proceeded forthwith to congratulate him as the author of a novel by Randolph Tomkins, whom he abominated most of all living writers.

Presently there was a stir in the company, those of the balcony came trooping into the drawing-room, four or five young men and girls, surrounding a tall woman in a black walking-dress; people dropped in to these open evenings of Mrs. Vanderwerf's from their row on the lagoon or stroll at St. Mark's.

Miss Vanderwerf jumped up.

"You aren't surely going yet, dearest?" she cried effusively. "My darling child, it isn't half-past ten yet."

"I must go; poor Gerty's in bed with a cold, and I must go and look after her."

"Bother Gerty!" ejaculated one of the well turned out æsthetic young men.

The tall young woman gave him what Marion noted as a shutting-up look.

"Learn to respect my belongings," she answered, "I must really go back to my cousin."

Jervase Marion had immediately identified her as the owner of that rather masculine voice with the falsetto tone; and apart from the voice, he would have identified her as the lady who had bullied the poor young man in distress about his sideboard. She was very tall, straight, and strongly built, the sort of woman whom you instinctively think of as dazzlingly fine in a ball frock; but at the same time active and stalwart, suggestive of long rides and drives and walks. She had handsome aquiline features, just a trifle wooden in their statuesque fineness, abundant fair hair, and a complexion, pure pink and white, which told of superb health. Marion knew the type well. It was one which, despite all the years he had lived in England, made him feel American, impressing him as something almost exotic. This great strength, size, cleanness of outline and complexion, this look of carefully selected breed, of carefully fostered health, was to him the perfect flower of the aristocratic civilization of England. There were more beautiful types, certainly, and, intellectually, higher ones (his experience was that such women were shrewd, practical, and quite deficient in soul), but there was no type more well-defined and striking, in his eyes. This woman did not seem an individual at all.

"I must go," insisted the tall lady, despite the prayers of her hostess and the assembled guests. "I really can't leave that poor creature alone a minute longer."

"Order the gondola, Kennedy; call Titta, please," cried Miss Vanderwerf to one of the many youths whom the kindly old maid ordered about with motherly familiarity.

"Mayn't I have the honour of offering mine?" piped the young man.

"Thanks, it isn't worth while. I shall walk." Here came a chorus of protestations, following the tall young woman into the outer drawing-room, through the hall, to the head of the great flight of open-air stairs.

Marion had mechanically followed the noisy, squabbling, laughing crew. The departure of this lady suggested to him that he would slip away to his inn.

"Do let me have the pleasure of accompanying you," cried one young man after another.

"*Do* take Clarence or Kennedy or Piccinillo, darling," implored Mrs. Vanderwerf. "You can't really walk home alone."

"It's not three steps from here," answered the tall one. "And I'm sure it's much more proper for a matron of ever so many years standing to go home alone than accompanied by a lot of fascinating young creatures."

"But, dear, you really don't know Venice; suppose you were spoken to! Just think."

"Well, beloved friend, I know enough Italian to be able to answer."

The tall lady raised one beautifully pencilled eyebrow, slightly, with a contemptuous little look. "Besides, I'm big enough to defend myself, and see, here's an umbrella with a silver knob, or what passes for such in these degenerate days. Nobody will come near that."

And she took the weapon from a rack in the hall, where the big seventeenth-century lamp flickered on the portraits of doges in crimson and senators in ermine.

"As you like, dearest. I know that wilful must have her own way," sighed Miss Vanderwerf, rising on tiptoe and kissing her on both cheeks.

"Mayn't I really accompany you?" repeated the various young men.

She shook her head, with the tall, pointed hat on it.

"No, you mayn't; good-night, dear friends," and she brandished her umbrella over her head and descended the stairs, which went sheer down into the moonlit yard. The young men bowed. One, with the air of a devotee in St. Mark's, kissed her hand at the bottom of the flight of steps, while the gondolier unlocked the gate. They could see him standing in the moonlight and hear him say earnestly:

"I leave for Paris to-morrow; good-night."

She did not answer him, but making a gesture with her umbrella to those above, she cried: "Good-night."

"Good-night," answered the chorus above the stairs, watching the tall figure pass beneath the gate and into the moonlit square.

"Well now," said Miss Vanderwerf, settling herself on her ottoman again, and fanning herself after her exertions in the drawing-room, "there is no denying that she's a strange creature, dear thing."

"A fine figure-head cut out of oak, with a good, solid, wooden heart," said the Roumanian Princess.

"No, no," exclaimed the lady of the house. "She's just as good as gold,—poor Lady Tal!"

II.

"Tal?" asked Marion.

"Tal. Her name's Atalanta, Lady Atalanta Walkenshaw—but everyone calls her Tal—Lady Tal. She's the daughter of Lord Ossian, you know."

"And who is or was Walkenshaw?—is, I presume, otherwise she'd have married somebody else by this time."

"Poor Tal!" mused Miss Vanderwerf. "I'm sure she would have no difficulty in finding another husband to make up for that fearful old Walkenshaw creature. But she's in a very sad position for so young a creature, poor girl."

"Ah!" ejaculated Marion, familiar with ladies thus to be commiserated, and remembering his friend's passion for romance, unquenchable by many seriocomic disenchantments, "separated from her husband—that sort of thing! I thought so."

"Now, why did you think that, you horrid creature?" asked his hostess eagerly. "Well, now, there's no saying that you're not *real* psychological, Jervase. Now *do* tell what made you think of such a thing."

"I don't know, I'm sure," answered Marion, suppressing a yawn. He hated people who pried into his novelist consciousness, all the more so that he couldn't in the least explain its contents. "Something about her—or nothing about her—a mere guess, a stupid random shot that happens to have hit right."

"Why, that's just the thing, that you haven't hit quite right. That is, it's right in one way, and wrong in another. Oh, my! how difficult it is just to explain, when one isn't a clever creature like you? Well, Lady Tal isn't separated from her husband, but it's just the same as if she were——;"

"I see. Mad? Poor thing!" exclaimed Marion with that air of concern which always left you in doubt whether it was utterly conventional, or might not contain a grain of sympathy after all.

"No, he's not mad. He's dead—been dead ever so long. She's one and thirty, you know—doesn't look it, does she?—and was married at eighteen. But she can't marry again, for all that, because if she marries all his money goes elsewhere, and she's not a penny to bless herself with."

"Ah—and why didn't she have proper settlements made?" asked Marion.

"That's just it. Because old Walkenshaw, who was a beast—just a beast—had a prejudice against settlements, and said he'd do much better for his wife than that—leave her everything, if only they didn't plague him. And then, when the old wretch died, after they'd been married a year or so, it turned out that he had left her everything, but only on condition of her not marrying again. If she did, it would all go to the next of kin. He hated the next of kin, too, they say, and wanted to keep the money away from him as long as possible, horrid old wretch! So there poor Tal is a widow, but unable to marry again."

"Dear me!" ejaculated Marion, looking at the patterns which the moonlight, falling between the gothic balcony balustrade, was making on the shining marble floor; and reflecting upon the neat way in which the late Walkenshaw had repaid his wife for marrying him for his money; for of course she had married him for his money. Marion was not a stoic, or a cynic, or a philosopher of any kind. He fully accepted the fact that the daughters of Scotch lords should marry for money, he even hated all sorts of sentimental twaddle about human dignity. But he rather sympathised with this old Walkenshaw, whoever Walkenshaw might have been, who had just served a mercenary young lady as was right.

"I don't see that it's so hard, aunt," said Miss Vanderwerf's niece, who was deeply in love with Bill Nettle, a penniless etcher. "Lady Tal might marry again if she'd learn to do without all that money."

"If she would be satisfied with only a little less," interrupted the sharp-featured Parisian-American whom Mrs. Vanderwerf wanted for a nephew-in-law. "Why, there are dozens of men with plenty of money who have been wanting to marry her. There was Sir Titus Farrinder, only last year. He mayn't have had as much as old Walkenshaw, but he had a jolly bit of money, certainly."

"Besides, after all," put in the millionaire in distraction about the sideboard, "why should Lady Tal want to marry again? She's got a lovely house at Rome."

"Oh, come, come, Clarence!" interrupted Kennedy horrified; "why, it's nothing but Japanese leather paper and Chinese fans."

"I don't know," said Clarence, crestfallen. "Perhaps it isn't lovely. I thought it *rather* pretty—don't you really think it *rather* nice, Miss Vanderwerf?"

"Any house would be nice enough with such a splendid creature inside it," put in Marion. These sort of conversations always interested him; it was the best way of studying human nature.

"Besides," remarked the Roumanian Princess, "Lady Tal may have had enough of the married state. And why indeed should a beautiful creature like that get married? She's got every one at her feet. It's much more amusing like that——;"

"Well, all the same, I *do* think it's just terribly sad, to see a creature like that condemned to lead such a life, without anyone to care for or protect her, now poor Gerald Burne's dead."

"Oh, her brother—her brother—do you suppose she cared for *him*?" asked the niece, pouring out the iced lemonade and Cyprus wine. She always rebelled against her aunt's romanticalness.

"Gerald Burne!" said Marion, collecting his thoughts, and suddenly seeing in his mind a certain keen-featured face, a certain wide curl of blond hair, not seen for many a long year. "Gerald Burne! Do you mean an awfully handsome young Scotchman, who did something very distinguished in Afghanistan? You don't mean to say he was any relation of Lady Atalanta's? I never heard of his being dead, either. I thought he must be somewhere in India."

"Gerald Burne was Lady Tal's half-brother—her mother had married a Colonel Burne before her marriage with Lord Ossian. He got a spear-wound or something out in Afghanistan," explained one of the company.

"I thought it was his horse," interrupted another.

"Anyhow," resumed Miss Vanderwerf, "poor Gerald was crippled for life— a sort of spinal disease, you know. That was just after old Sir Thomas Walkenshaw departed, so Tal and he lived together and went travelling from one place to another, consulting doctors, and that sort of thing, until they settled in Rome. And now poor Gerald is dead—he died two years ago— Tal's all alone in the world, for Lord Ossian's a wretched, tipsy, bankrupt old creature, and the other sisters are married. Gerald was just an angel, and you've no idea how devoted poor Tal was to him—he was just her life, I do believe."

The young man called Ted looked contemptuously at his optimistic hostess.

"Well," he said, "I don't know whether Lady Tal cared much for her brother while he was alive. My belief is she never cared a jackstraw for anyone. Anyway, if she *did* care for him you must admit she didn't show it after his death. I never saw a woman look so utterly indifferent and heartless as when I saw her a month later. She made jokes, I remember, and asked me to take her to a curiosity shop. And she went to balls in London not a year afterwards."

The niece nodded. "Exactly. I always thought it perfectly indecent. Of course Aunt says it's Tal's way of showing her grief, but it's a very funny one, anyhow."

"I'm sure Lady Tal must regret her brother," said the Roumanian Princess. "Just think how convenient for a young widow to be able to say to all the men she likes: 'Oh, do come and see poor Gerald.'"

"Well, well!" remarked Miss Vanderwerf. "Of course she did take her brother's death in a very unusual way. But still I maintain she's not heartless for all that."

"Hasn't a pretty woman a right to be heartless, after all?" put in Marion.

"Oh, I don't care a fig whether Lady Tal is heartless or not," answered Ted brusquely. "Heartlessness isn't a social offence. What I object to most in Lady Tal is her being so frightfully mean."

"Mean?"

"Why, yes; avaricious. With all those thousands, that woman manages to spend barely more than a few hundreds."

"Well, but if she's got simple tastes?" suggested Marion.

"She hasn't. No woman was ever further from it. And of course it's so evident what her game is! She just wants to feather her nest against a rainy day. She's putting by five-sixths of old Walkenshaw's money, so as to make herself a nice little *dot*, to marry someone else upon one of these days."

"A judicious young lady!" observed Marion.

"Well, really, Mr. Kennedy," exclaimed the Roumanian Princess, "you are ingenious and ingenuous! Do you suppose that our dear Tal is putting by money in order to marry some starving genius, to do love in a cottage with? Why, if she's not married yet, it's merely because she's not met a sufficient *parti*. She wants something very grand—a *Pezzo Grosso*, as they say here."

"She couldn't marry as long as she had Gerald to look after," said Miss Vanderwerf, fanning herself in the moonlight. "She was too fond of Gerald."

"She was afraid of Gerald, that's my belief, too," corrected the niece. "Those big creatures are always cowards. And Gerald hated the notion of her making another money marriage, though he seems to have arranged pretty well to live on old Walkenshaw's thousands."

"Of course Gerald wanted to keep her all for himself; that was quite natural," said Miss Vanderwerf; "but I think that as long as he was alive she did not want anyone else. She thought only of him, poor creature——;"

"And of a score of ball and dinner-parties and a few hundred acquaintances," put in Ted, making rings with the smoke of his cigarette.

"And now," said the Princess, "she's waiting to find her *Pezzo Grosso*. And she wants money because she knows that a *Pezzo Grosso* will marry a penniless girl of eighteen, but won't marry a penniless woman of thirty; she must make up for being a little *passée* by loving him for his own sake, and for that, she must have money."

"For all that, poor Tal's very simple," wheezed the old peeress, apparently awakening from a narcotic slumber. "She always reminds me of an anecdote poor dear Palmerston used to tell——;"

"Anyhow," said Kennedy, "Lady Tal's a riddle, and I pity the man who tries to guess it. Good-night, dear Miss Vanderwerf—good-night, Miss Bessy. It's all settled about dining at the Lido, I hope. And you'll come, too, I hope, Mr. Marion."

"I'll come with pleasure, particularly if you ask the enigmatic Lady Tal."

"Much good it is to live in Venice," thought Jervase Marion, looking out of his window on to the canal, "if one spends two hours discussing a young woman six foot high looking out for a duke."

III.

Jervase Marion had registered three separate, well-defined, and solemn vows, which I recapitulate in the inverse order to their importance. The first was: Not to be enticed into paying calls during that month at Venice; the second, Not to drift into studying any individual character while on a holiday; and the third, a vow dating from more years back than he cared to think of, and resulting from infinite bitterness of spirit, Never to be entrapped, beguiled, or bullied into looking at the manuscript of an amateur novelist. And now he had not been in Venice ten days before he had broken each of these vows in succession; and broken them on behalf, too, of one and the same individual.

The individual in question was Lady Atalanta Walkenshaw, or, as he had already got accustomed to call her, Lady Tal. He had called upon Lady Tal; he had begun studying Lady Tal; and now he was actually untying the string which fastened Lady Tal's first attempt at a novel.

Why on earth had he done any of these things, much less all? Jervase Marion asked himself, leaving the folded parcel unopened on the large round table, covered with a black and red table-cloth, on which were neatly spread out his writing-case, blotter, inkstand, paper-cutter, sundry packets of envelopes, and boxes of cigarettes, two uncut *Athenæums*, three dog-eared French novels (Marion secretly despised all English ones, and was for ever coveting that exquisite artistic sense, that admirable insincerity of the younger Frenchmen), a Baedeker, a Bradshaw, the photograph, done just before her death, of his mother in her picturesque, Puritan-looking widow's cap, and a little portfolio for unanswered letters, with flowers painted on it by his old friend, Biddy Lothrop.

Marion gave the parcel, addressed in a large, quill-pen hand, a look of utter despair, and thrusting his hands ungracefully but desperately into the armhole of his alpaca writing-jacket, paced slowly up and down his darkened room on a side canal. He had chosen that room, rather than one on the Riva, thinking it would be less noisy. But it seemed to him now, in one of his nervous fits, as if all the noises of the world had concentrated on to that side canal to distract his brain, weaken his will, and generally render him incapable of coping with his own detestable weakness and Lady Tal's terrible determination. There was a plash of oar, a grind of keel, in that side canal, a cry of *Stali* or *Premè* from the gondoliers, only the more worrying for its comparative rareness. There was an exasperating blackbird who sang Garibaldi's hymn, in separate fragments, a few doors off, and an even more exasperating kitchen-maid, who sang the first bars of the umbrella trio of *Boccaccio*, without getting any further, while scouring her brasses at the window opposite, and rinsing out her saucepans, with a furtive splash into the canal. There was the bugle of the barracks, the bell of the parish church, the dog yelping on the boats of the Riva; everything in short which could madden a poor nervous novelist who has the crowning misfortune of looking delightfully placid.

Why on earth, or rather how on earth, had he let himself in for all this? "All this" being the horrible business of Lady Atalanta, the visits to pay her, the manuscript to read, the judgment to pass, the advice to give, the lies to tell, all vaguely complicated with the song of that blackbird, the jar of that gondola keel, the jangle of those church bells. How on earth could he have been such a miserable worm? Marion asked himself, pacing up and down his large, bare room, mopping his head, and casting despairing glances at the mosquito curtains, the bulging yellow chest of drawers painted over with nosegays, the iron clothes-horse, the towel-stand, the large printed card setting forth in various tongues the necessity of travellers consigning all jewels and valuables to the secretary of the hotel at the Bureau.

He could not, at present, understand in the very least why he had given that young woman any encouragement; for he must evidently have given her some encouragement before she could have gone to the length of asking so great a favour of a comparative stranger. And the odd part of it was, that when he looked into the past, that past of a few days only, it seemed as if, so far from his having encouraged Lady Tal, it had been Lady Tal who had encouraged him. He saw her, the more he looked, in the attitude of a woman granting a favour, not asking one. He couldn't even explain to himself how the matter of the novel had ever come up. He certainly couldn't remember having said: "I wish you would let me see your novel, Lady Tal," or "I should be curious to have a look at that novel of yours;" such a thing would have been too absurd on the part of a man who had always fled from manuscripts as from the plague. At the same time he seemed to have no recollection either of her having said the other thing, the more or less humble request for a reading. He recollected her saying: "Mind you tell me the exact truth—and don't be afraid of telling me if it's all disgusting rubbish." Indeed he could see something vaguely amused, mischievous, and a little contemptuous in the handsome, regular Scotch face; but that had been afterwards, after he had already settled the matter with her.

It was the sense of having been got the better of, and in a wholly unintelligible way, which greatly aggravated the matter. For Marion did not feel the very faintest desire to do Lady Atalanta a service. He would not have minded so much if she had wheedled him into it,—no man thinks the worse of himself for having been wheedled by a handsome young woman of fashion,—or if she had been an appealing or pathetic creature, one of those who seem to suggest that this is just all that can be done for them, and that perhaps one may regret not having done it over their early grave.

Lady Tal was not at all an appealing woman; she looked three times as strong, both in body and in mind, with her huge, strongly-knit frame, and clear, pink complexion, and eyes which evaded you, as himself and most of his acquaintances. And as to wheedling, how could she wheedle, this woman with her rather angular movements, brusque, sarcastic, bantering speech, and look of counting all the world as dust for an Ossian to trample underfoot? Moreover, Marion was distinctly aware of the fact that he rather disliked Lady Tal. It was not anything people said about her (although they seemed to say plenty), nor anything she said herself; it was a vague repulsion due to her dreadful strength, her appearance of never having felt anything, the hardness of those blue, bold eyes, the resolution of that well-cut, firmly closing mouth, the bantering tone of that voice, and the consequent impression which she left on him of being able to take care of herself to an extent almost dangerous to her fellow-creatures. Marion was not a sentimental novelist; his books turned mainly upon the little intrigues and struggles of the highly civilized portion of society, in which only the fittest have survived, by virtue of talon and beak. Yet he owned to himself, in the presence of Lady Atalanta Walkenshaw, or rather behind her back, that he did like human beings, and especially women, to have a soul; implying thereby that the lady in question affected him as being hampered by no such impediment to digestion, sleep, and worldly distinction.

It was this want of soul which constituted the strength of Lady Tal. This negative quality had much more than the value of a positive one. And it was Lady Tal's want of soul which had, somehow, got the better of him, pushed him, bullied him, without any external manifestation, and by a mere hidden force, into accepting, or offering to read that manuscript.

Jervase Marion was a methodical man, full of unformulated principles of existence. One of these consisted in always doing unpleasant duties at once, unless they were so unpleasant that he never did them at all. Accordingly, after a turn or two more up and down the room, and a minute or two lolling out of the window, and looking into that kitchen on the other side of the canal, with the bright saucepans in the background, and the pipkins with carnations and sweet basil on the sill, Marion cut the strings of the manuscript, rolled it backwards to make it lie flat, and with a melancholy little moan, began reading Lady Tal's novel.

"Violet——;" it began.

"Violet! and her name's Violet too!" ejaculated Marion to himself.

"Violet is seated in a low chair in the gloom in the big bow window at Kieldar—the big bow window encircled by ivy and constructed it is said by Earl Rufus before he went to the crusades and from which you command a magnificent prospect of the broad champaign country extending for many miles, all dotted with oaks and farmhouses and bounded on the horizon by the blue line of the hills of B——;shire—the window in which she had sat so often and cried as a child when her father Lord Rufus had married again and brought home that handsome Jewish wife with the *fardée* face and the exquisite dresses from Worth—Violet had taken refuge in that window in order to think over the events of the previous evening and that offer of marriage which her cousin Marmaduke had just made to her——;"

"Bless the woman!" exclaimed Marion, "what on earth is it all about?" And he registered the remark, to be used upon the earliest occasion in one of his own novels, that highly-connected and well-dressed young women of the present generation, appear to leave commas and semicolons, all in fact except full stops and dashes, to their social inferiors.

The remark consoled him, also, by its practical bearing on the present situation, for it would enable him to throw the weight of his criticisms on this part of Lady Tal's performance.

"You must try, my dear Lady Atalanta," he would say very gravely, "to cultivate a—a—somewhat more lucid style—to cut down your sentences a little—in fact to do what we pedantic folk call break up the members of a period. In order to do so, you must turn your attention very seriously to the subject of punctuation, which you seem to have—a—well—rather neglected hitherto. I will send for an invaluable little work on the subject—'Stops: and how to manage them,' which will give you all necessary information. Also, if you can find it in the library of any of our friends here, I should recommend your studying a book which I used in my boyhood,—a great many years ago, alas!—called 'Blair's Rhetoric.'"

If that didn't quench Lady Tal's literary ardour, nothing ever would. But all the same he felt bound to read on a little, in order to be able to say he had done so.

IV.

Jervase Marion fixed his eyes, the eyes of the spirit particularly, upon Lady Tal, as he sat opposite her, the next day, at the round dinner table, in Palazzo Bragadin.

He was trying to make out how on earth this woman had come to write the novel he had been reading. That Lady Tal should possess considerable knowledge of the world, and of men and women, did not surprise him in the least. He had recognised, in the course of various conversations, that this young lady formed an exception to the rule that splendid big creatures with regular features and superb complexions are invariably idiots.

That Lady Tal should even have a certain talent—about as cultivated as that of the little boys who draw horses on their copy books—for plot and dialogue, was not astonishing at all, any more than that her sentences invariably consisted either of three words, or of twenty-seven lines, and that her grammar and spelling were nowhere. All this was quite consonant with Lady Tal's history, manner, talk, and with that particular beauty of hers—the handsome aquiline features, too clean-cut for anything save wood or stone, the bright, cold, blue eyes, which looked you in the face when you expected it least, and which looked away from you when you expected it least, also; the absence of any of those little subtle lines which tell of feeling and thought, and which complete visible beauty, while suggesting a beauty transcending mere visible things. There was nothing at all surprising in this. But Jervase Marion had found in this manuscript something quite distinct and unconnected with such matters: he had found the indications of a soul, a very decided and unmistakable soul.

And now, looking across the fruit and flowers, and the set out of old Venetian glass on Miss Vanderwerf's hospitable table, he asked himself in what portion of the magnificent person of Lady Atalanta Walkenshaw that soul could possibly be located.

Lady Tal was seated, as I have remarked, immediately opposite Marion, and between a rather battered cosmopolitan diplomatist and the young millionaire who had been in distress about a sideboard. Further along was the Roumanian Princess, and opposite, on the other side of Marion, an elderly American siren, in an extremely simple white muslin frock, at the first glance the work of the nursery maid, at the second of Worth, and symbolising the strange, dangerous fascination of a lady whom you took at first for a Puritan and a frump. On the other sat Miss Gertrude Ossian, Lady Tal's cousin, a huge young woman with splendid arms and shoulders and atrocious manners, who thought Venice such a bore because it was too hot to play at tennis and you couldn't ride on canals, and consoled herself by attempting to learn the guitar from various effete Italian youths, whom she alarmed and delighted in turn.

Among this interesting company Lady Tal was seated with that indefinable look of being a great deal too large, too strong, too highly connected, and too satisfied with herself and all things, for this miserable, effete, plebeian, and self-conscious universe.

She wore a beautifully-made dress of beautifully-shining silk, and her shoulders and throat and arms were as beautifully made and as shining as her dress; and her blond hair was as elaborately and perfectly arranged as it was possible to conceive. That blond hair, verging upon golden, piled up in smooth and regular plaits and rolls till it formed a kind of hard and fantastic helmet about her very oval face, and arranged in a close row of symmetrical little curls upon the high, white, unmarked forehead, and about the thin, black, perfectly-arched eyebrows—that hair of Lady Tal's symbolised, in the thought of Marion, all that was magnificent, conventional, and impassive in this creature. Those blue eyes also, which looked at you and away from you, when you expected each least, were too large, under the immense arch of eyebrow, to do more than look out indifferently upon the world. The mouth was too small in its beautiful shape for any contraction or expression of feeling, and when she smiled, those tiny white teeth seemed still to shut it. And altogether, with its finely-moulded nostrils, which were never dilated, and its very oval outline, the whole face affected Marion as a huge and handsome mask, as something clapped on and intended to conceal. To conceal what? It seemed to the novelist, as he listened to the stream of animated conventionalities, of jokes unconnected with any high spirits, that the mask of Lady Atalanta's face, like those great stone masks in Roman galleries and gardens, concealed the mere absence of everything. As Marion contemplated Lady Tal, he reviewed mentally that manuscript novel written in a hand as worn down as that of a journalist, and with rather less grammar and spelling than might be expected from a nursery maid; and he tried to connect the impression it had left on his mind with the impression which its author was making at the present moment.

The novel had taken him by surprise by its subject, and even more by its particular moral attitude. The story was no story at all, merely the unnoticed martyrdom of a delicate and scrupulous woman tied to a vain, mean, and frivolous man; the long starvation of a little soul which required affections and duties among the unrealities of the world. Not at all an uncommon subject nowadays; in fact, Marion could have counted you off a score of well-known novels on similar or nearly similar themes.

There was nothing at all surprising in the novel, the surprising point lay in its having this particular author.

Little by little, as the impression of the book became fainter, and the impression of the writer more vivid, Marion began to settle his psychological problem. Or rather he began to settle that there was no psychological problem at all. This particular theme was in vogue nowadays, this particular moral view was rife in the world; Lady Tal had read other people's books, and had herself written a book which was extremely like theirs. It was a case of unconscious, complete imitation. The explanation of Lady Tal's having produced a novel so very different from herself, was simply that, as a matter of fact, she had not produced that novel at all. It was unlike herself because it belonged to other people, that was all.

"Tell me about my novel," she said after dinner, beckoning Marion into one of the little gothic balconies overhanging the grand canal; the little balconies upon whose cushions and beneath whose drawn-up awning there is room for two, just out of earshot of any two others on the other balconies beyond.

Places for flirtation. But Lady Tal, Marion had instinctively understood, was not a woman who flirted. Her power over men, if she had any, or chose to exert it, must be of the sledge-hammer sort. And how she could possibly have any power over anything save a mere gaping masher, over anything that had, below its starched shirt front, sensitiveness, curiosity, and imagination, Marion at this moment utterly failed to understand.

The tone of this woman's voice, the very rustle of her dress, as she leaned upon the balcony and shook the sparks from her cigarette into the dark sky and the dark water, seemed to mean business and nothing but business.

She said:

"Tell me all about my novel. I don't intend to be put off with mere remarks about grammar and stops. One may learn all about that; or can't all that, and style, and so forth, be put in for one, by the printer's devil? I haven't a very clear notion what a printer's devil is, except that he's a person with a thumb. But he might see to such details, or somebody else of the same sort."

"Quite so. A novelist of some slight established reputation would do as well, Lady Tal."

Marion wondered why he had made that answer; Lady Tal's remark was impertinent only inasmuch as he chose to admit that she could be impertinent to him.

Lady Tal, he felt, but could not see, slightly raised one of those immensely curved eyebrows of hers in the darkness.

"I thought that you, for instance, might get me through all that," she answered; "or some other novelist, as you say, of established reputation, who *was* benevolently inclined towards a poor, helpless ignoramus with literary aspirations."

"Quite apart from such matters—and you are perfectly correct in supposing that there must be lots of professed novelists who would most gladly assist you with them—quite apart from such matters, your novel, if you will allow me to say a rude thing, is utterly impossible. You are perpetually taking all sorts of knowledge for granted in your reader. Your characters don't sufficiently explain themselves; you write as if your reader had witnessed the whole thing and merely required reminding. I almost doubt whether you have fully realized for yourself a great part of the situation; one would think you were repeating things from hearsay, without quite understanding them."

Marion felt a twinge of conscience: that wasn't the impression left by the novel, but the impression due to the discrepancy between the novel and its author. That hateful habit of studying people, of turning them round, prodding and cutting them to see what was inside, why couldn't he leave it behind for awhile? Had he not come to Venice with the avowed intention of suspending all such studies?

Lady Tal laughed. The laugh was a little harsh. "You say that because of the modelling of my face—I know all about modelling of faces, and facial angles, and cheek-bones, and eye cavities: I once learned to draw—people always judge of me by the modelling of my face. Perhaps they are right, perhaps they are wrong. I daresay I *have* taken too much for granted. One ought never to take anything for granted, in the way of human insight, ought one? Anyhow, perhaps you will show me when I have gone wrong, will you?"

"It will require a good deal of patience——;" began Marion.

"On your part, of course. But then it all turns to profit with you novelists; and it's men's business to be patient, just because they never are."

"I meant on your part, Lady Tal. I question whether you have any notion of what it means to recast a novel—to alter it throughout, perhaps not only once, but twice, or three times."

"Make me a note of the main wrongness, and send me the MS., will you? I'll set about altering it at once, you'll see. I'm a great deal more patient than you imagine, Mr. Marion, when I want a thing—and I do want this—I want to write novels. I want the occupation, the interest, the excitement. Perhaps some day I shall want the money too. One makes pots of money in your business, doesn't one?"

Lady Atalanta laughed. She threw her cigarette into the canal, and with a crackle and a rustle of her light dress, straightened her huge person, and after looking for a moment into the blue darkness full of dim houses and irregularly scattered lights, she swept back into the hum of voices and shimmer of white dresses of Miss Vanderwerf's big drawing-room.

Jervase Marion remained leaning on the balcony, listening to the plash of oar and the bursts of hoarse voices and shrill fiddles from the distant music boats.

V.

The temptations of that demon of psychological study proved too great for Marion; particularly when that tempter allied himself to an equally stubborn though less insidious demon apparently residing in Lady Atalanta: the demon of amateur authorship. So that, by the end of ten days, there was established, between Lady Tal's lodgings and Marion's hotel, a lively interchange of communication, porters and gondoliers for ever running to and fro between "that usual tall young lady at San Vio," and "that usual short, bald gentleman on the Riva." The number of parcels must have been particularly mysterious to these messengers, unless the proverbially rapid intuition (inherited during centuries of intrigue and spying) of Venetian underlings arrived at the fact that the seemingly numberless packets were in reality always one and the same, or portions of one and the same: the celebrated novel travelling to and fro, with perpetual criticisms from Marion and corrections from Lady Atalanta. This method of intercourse was, however, daily supplemented by sundry notes, in the delicate, neat little hand of the novelist, or the splashing writing of the lady, saying with little variation—"Dear Lady Atalanta, I fear I may not have made my meaning very clear with respect to Chapter I, II, III, IV—or whatever it might be—will you allow me to give you some verbal explanations on the subject?" and "Dear Mr. Marion,—*Do* come *at once.* I've got stuck over that beastly chapter V, VI, or VII, and positively *must* see you about it."

"Well, I never!" politely ejaculated Miss Vanderwerf regularly every evening—"if that Marion isn't the most *really* kind and patient creature on this earth!"

To which her friend the Princess, the other arbitress of Venetian society in virtue of her palace, her bric-à-brac, and that knowledge of Marie Corelli and

Mrs. Campbell-Praed which balanced Miss Vanderwerf's capacity for grasping the meaning of Gyp—invariably answered in her best English colloquial:

"Well, my word! If that Lady Tal's not the most impudent amateur scribble-scrabble of all the amateur scribble-scrabbles that England produces."

Remarks which immediately produced a lively discussion of Lady Tal and of Marion, including the toilettes of the one and the books of the other, with the result that neither retained a single moral, intellectual, or physical advantage; and the obvious corollary, in the mind of the impartial listener, that Jervase Marion evidently gave up much more of his time to Lady Tal and her novel than to Miss Vanderwerf and the Princess and their respective salons.

As a matter of fact, however, although a degree of impudence more politely described as energy and determination, on the part of Lady Tal; and of kindness, more correctly designated as feebleness of spirit, on the part of Marion, had undoubtedly been necessary in the first stages of this intercourse, yet nothing of either of these valuable social qualities had been necessary for its continuation. Although maintaining that manner of hers expressive of the complete rights which her name of Ossian and her additional inches constituted over all things and people, Lady Tal had become so genuinely enthusiastic for the novelist's art as revealed by Marion, that her perpetual intrusion upon his leisure was that merely of an ardent if somewhat inconsiderate disciple. In the eyes of this young lady, development of character, foreshortening of narrative, construction, syntax, nay, even grammar and punctuation, had become inexhaustible subjects of meditation and discussion, upon which every experience of life could be brought to bear.

So much for Lady Tal. As regards Marion, he had, not without considerable self-contempt, surrendered himself to the demon of character study. This passion for investigating into the feelings and motives of his neighbours was at once the joy, the pride, and the bane and humiliation of Marion's placid life. He was aware that he had, for years and years, cultivated this tendency to the utmost; and he was fully convinced that to study other folks and embody his studies in the most lucid form was the one mission of his life, and a mission in nowise inferior to that of any other highly gifted class of creatures. Indeed, if Jervase Marion, ever since his earliest manhood, had given way to a tendency to withdraw from all personal concerns, from all emotion or action, it was mainly because he conceived that this shrinkingness of nature (which foolish persons called egoism) was the necessary complement to his power of intellectual analysis; and that any departure from the position of dispassioned spectator of the world's follies and miseries would mean also a departure from his real duty as a novelist. To be brought into contact with people more closely than was necessary or advantageous for their intellectual comprehension; to think about them, feel about them, mistress, wife, son, or daughter, the bare thought of such a thing jarred upon Marion's nerves. So, the better to study, the better to be solitary, he had expatriated himself, leaving brothers, sisters (now his mother was dead), friends of childhood, all those things which invade a man's consciousness without any psychological profit; he had condemned himself to live in a world of acquaintances, of indifference; and, for sole diversion, he permitted himself, every now and then, to come abroad to places where he had not even acquaintances, where he could look at faces which had no associations for him, and speculate upon the character of total strangers. Only, being a methodical man, and much concerned for his bodily and intellectual health, he occasionally thought fit to suspend even this contact with mankind, and to spend six weeks, as he had intended spending those six weeks at Venice, in the contemplation of only bricks and mortar.

And now, that demon of psychological study had got the better of his determination. Marion understood it all now from the beginning: that astonishing feebleness of his towards Lady Atalanta, that extraordinary submission to this imperious and audacious young aristocrat's orders. The explanation was simple, though curious. He had divined in Lady Atalanta a very interesting psychological problem, considerably before he had been able to formulate the fact to himself: his novelist's intuition, like the scent of a dog, had set him on the track even before he knew the nature of the game, or the desire to pursue. Before even beginning to think about Lady Atalanta, he had begun to watch her; he was watching her now consciously; indeed all his existence was engrossed in such watching, so that the hours he spent away from her company, or the company of her novel, were so many gaps in his life.

Jervase Marion, as a result both of that shrinkingness of nature, and of a very delicate artistic instinct, had an aversion of such coarse methods of study as consist in sitting down in front of a human being and staring, in a metaphorical sense, at him or her. He was not a man of theories (their cut-and-driedness offending his subtlety); but had he been forced to formulate his ideas, he would have said that in order to perceive the real values (in pictorial language) of any individual, you must beware of isolating him or her; you must merely look attentively at the moving ocean of human faces, watching for the one face more particularly interesting than the rest, and catching glimpses of its fleeting expression, and of the expression of its neighbours as it appears and reappears. Perhaps, however, Marion's other reason against the sit-down-and-stare or walk-round-and-pray system of psychological study was really the stronger one in his nature, the more so that he would probably not have admitted its superior validity. This other reason was a kind of moral scruple against getting to know the secret mechanism of a soul, especially if such knowledge involved an appearance of intimacy with a person in whom he could never take more than a merely abstract, artistic interest. It was a mean taking advantage of superior strength, or the raising of expectations which could not be fulfilled; for Marion, although the most benevolent and serviceable of mortals, did not give his heart, perhaps because he had none to give, to anybody.

This scruple had occurred to Marion almost as soon as he discovered himself to be studying Lady Tal; and it occurred to him once or twice afterwards. But he despatched it satisfactorily. Lady Tal, in the first place, was making use of him in the most outrageous way, without scruple or excuse; it was only just that he, in his turn, should turn her to profit with equal freedom. This reason, however, savoured slightly of intellectual caddishness, and Marion rejected it with scorn. The real one, he came to perceive, was that Lady Tal gratuitously offered herself for study by her quiet, aggressive assumption of inscrutability. She really thrust her inscrutability down one's throat; her face, her manner, her every remark, her very novel, were all so many audacious challenges to the more psychological members of the community. She seemed to be playing on a gong and crying: "Does anyone feel inclined to solve a riddle? Is there any person who thinks himself sufficiently clever to understand me?" And when a woman takes up such an attitude, it is only natural, human and proper that the first novelist who comes along that way should stop and say: "I intend to get to the bottom of you; one, two, three, I am going to begin."

So Jervase Marion assiduously cultivated the society of Lady Atalanta, and spent most of his time instructing her in the art of the novelist.

VI.

One morning Marion, by way of exception, saw and studied Lady Tal without the usual medium of the famous novel. It was early, with the very first autumn crispness in the blue morning, in the bright sun which would soon burn, but as yet barely warmed. Marion was taking his usual ramble through the tortuous Venetian alleys, and as usual he had found himself in one of his favourite haunts, the market on the further slope of the Rialto.

That market—the yellow and white awnings, and the white houses against the delicate blue sky; the bales and festoons of red and green and blue and purple cotton stuffs outside the little shops, and below that the shawled women pattering down the bridge steps towards it; the monumental display of piled up peaches and pears, and heaped up pumpkins and mysterious unknown cognate vegetables, round and long, purple, yellow, red, grey, among the bay leaves, the great, huge, smooth, green-striped things, cut open to show their red pulp, the huger things looking as if nature had tried to gild and silver them unsuccessfully, tumbled on to the pavement; the butchers' shops with the gorgeous bullocks' hearts and sacrificial fleeced lambs; the endless hams and sausages—all this market, under the blue sky, with this lazy, active, noisy, brawling, friendly population jerking and lolling about it, always seemed to Marion one of the delightful spots of Venice, pleasing him with a sense (although he knew it to be all false) that here *was* a place where people could eat and drink and laugh and live without any psychological troubles.

On this particular morning, as this impression with the knowledge of its falseness was as usual invading Marion's consciousness, he experienced a little shock of surprise, incongruity, and the sudden extinction of a pleasingly unreal mood, on perceiving, coming towards him, with hand cavalierly on hip and umbrella firmly hitting the ground, the stately and faultlessly coated and shirted and necktied figure of Lady Atalanta.

"I have had a go already at *Christina*," she said, after extending to Marion an angular though friendly handshake, and a cheerful frank inscrutable smile of her big blue eyes and her little red mouth. "That novel is turning me into another woman: the power of sinning, as the Salvationists say, has been extracted out of my nature even by the rootlets; I sat up till two last night after returning from the Lido, and got up this morning at six, all for the love of *Christina* and literature. I expect Dawson will give me warning; she told me yesterday that she 'had never *know* any other lady that writes so much or used them big sheets of paper, quite *henormous*, my lady.' Dear old place, isn't it? Ever tasted any of that fried pumpkin? It's rather nasty but quite good; have some? I wonder we've not met here before; I come here twice a week to shop. You don't mind carrying parcels, do you?" Lady Tal had stopped at one of the front stalls, and having had three vast yellow paper bags filled with oranges and lemons, she handed the two largest to Marion.

"You'll carry them for me, won't you, there's a good creature: like that I shall be able to get rather more rolls than I usually can. It's astonishing how much sick folk care for rolls. I ought to explain I'm going to see some creatures at the hospital. It takes too long going there in the gondola from my place, so I walk. If you were to put those bags well on your chest like that, under your chin, they'd be easier to hold, and there'd be less chance of the oranges bobbing out."

At a baker's in one of the little narrow streets near the church of the Miracoli, Lady Atalanta provided herself with a bag of rolls, which she swung by the string to her wrist. Marion then perceived that she was carrying under her arm a parcel of paper-covered books, fastened with an elastic band.

"Now we shall have got everything except some flowers, which I daresay we can get somewhere on the way," remarked Lady Tal. "Do you mind coming in here?" and she entered one of those little grocer's shops, dignified with the arms of Savoy in virtue of the sale of salt and tobacco, and where a little knot of vague, wide-collared individuals usually hang about among the various-shaped liqueur bottles in an atmosphere of stale cigar, brandy and water, and kitchen soap.

"May—I—a—a—ask for anything for you, Lady Tal?" requested Marion, taken completely by surprise by the rapidity of his companion's movements. "You want stamps, I presume; may I have the honour of assisting you in your purchase?"

"Thanks, it isn't stamps; it's snuff, and you wouldn't know what sort to get." And Lady Tal, making her stately way through the crowd of surprised loafers, put a franc on the counter and requested the presiding female to give her four ounces of *Semolino*, but of the good sort——;"It's astonishing how faddy those old creatures are about their snuff!" remarked Lady Tal, pocketing her change. "Would you put this snuff in your pocket for me? Thanks. The other sort's called *Bacubino*, it's dark and clammy, and it looks nasty. Have you ever taken snuff? I do sometimes to please my old creatures; it makes me sneeze, you know, and they think that awful fun."

As they went along Lady Atalanta suddenly perceived, in a little green den, something which attracted her attention.

"I wonder whether they're fresh?" she mused. "I suppose you can't tell a fresh egg when you see it, can you, Mr. Marion? Never mind, I'll risk it. If you'll take this third bag of oranges, I'll carry the eggs—they might come to grief in your hands, you know."

"What an odious, odious creature a woman is," thought Marion. He wondered, considerably out of temper, why he should feel so miserable at having to carry all those oranges. Of course with three gaping bags piled on his chest there was the explanation of acute physical discomfort; but that wasn't sufficient. It seemed as if this terrible, aristocratic giantess were doing it all on purpose to make him miserable. He saw that he was intensely ridiculous in her eyes, with those yellow bags against his white waistcoat and the parcel of snuff in his coat pocket; his face was also, he thought, streaming with perspiration, and he couldn't get at his handkerchief. It was childish, absurd of him to mind; for, after all, wasn't Lady Atalanta equally burdened? But she, with her packets of rolls, and packet of books, and basket of eggs, and her umbrella tucked under her arm, looked serene and even triumphant in her striped flannel.

"I beg your pardon—would you allow me to stop a minute and shift the bags to the other arm?" Marion could no longer resist that fearful agony. "If you go on I'll catch you up in a second."

But just as Marion was about to rest the bags upon the marble balustrade of a bridge, his paralysed arm gave an unaccountable jerk, and out flew one of the oranges, and rolled slowly down the stone steps of the bridge.

"I say, don't do that! You'll have them all in the canal!" cried Lady Atalanta, as Marion quickly stooped in vain pursuit of the escaped orange, the movement naturally, and as if it were being done on purpose, causing another orange to fly out in its turn; a small number of spectators, gondoliers and workmen from under the bridge, women nursing babies at neighbouring windows, and barefooted urchins from nowhere in particular, starting up to enjoy the extraordinary complicated conjuring tricks which the stout gentleman in the linen coat and Panama hat had suddenly fallen to execute.

"Damn the beastly things!" ejaculated Marion, forgetful of Lady Atalanta and good breeding, and perceiving only the oranges jumping and rolling about, and feeling his face grow redder and hotter in the glare on that white stone bridge. At that moment, as he raised his eyes, he saw, passing along, a large party of Americans from his hotel; Americans whom he had avoided like the plague, who, he felt sure, would go home and represent him as a poor creature and a snob disavowing his "people." He could hear them, in fancy, describing how at Venice he had turned flunky to one of your English aristocrats, who stood looking and making game of him while he ran after her oranges, "and merely because she's the daughter of an Earl or Marquis or such like."

"Bless my heart, how helpless is genius when it comes to practical matters!" exclaimed Lady Atalanta. And putting her various packages down carefully on the parapet, she calmly collected the bounding oranges, wiped them with her handkerchief, and restored them to Marion, recommending him to "stick them loose in his pockets."

Marion had never been in a hospital (he had been only a boy, and in Europe with his mother, a Southern refugee, at the time of the War), the fact striking him as an omission in his novelist's education. But he felt as if he would never wish to describe the one into which he mechanically followed Lady Tal. With its immense, immensely lofty wards, filled with greyish light, and radiating like the nave and transepts of a vast church from an altar with flickering lights and kneeling figures, it struck Marion, while he breathed that hot, thick air, sickly with carbolic and chloride of lime, as a most gruesome and quite objectionably picturesque place. He had a vague notion that the creatures in the rows and rows of greyish white beds ought to have St. Vitus's dance or leprosy or some similar mediæval disease. They were nasty enough objects, he thought, as he timidly followed Lady Tal's rapid and resounding footsteps, for anything. He had, for all the prosaic quality of his writings, the easily roused imagination of a nervous man: and it seemed to him as if they were all of them either skeletons gibbering and screeching in bed, or frightful yellow and red tumid creatures, covered with plasters and ligatures, or old ladies recently liberated from the cellar in which, as you may periodically read in certain public prints, they had been kept by barbarous nephews or grandchildren——;

"Dear me, dear me, what a dreadful place!" he kept ejaculating, as he followed Lady Atalanta, carrying her bags of oranges and rolls, among the vociferating, grabbing beldames in bed, and the indifferent nuns and serving wenches toiling about noisily: Lady Tal going methodically her way, businesslike, cheerful, giving to one some snuff, to another an orange or a book, laughing, joking in her bad Italian, settling the creatures' disagreeable bed-clothes and pillows for them, as if instead of cosseting dying folk, she was going round to the counters of some huge shop. A most painful exhibition, thought Marion.

"I say, suppose you talk to her, she's a nice little commonplace creature who wanted to be a school-mistress and is awfully fond of reading novels—tell her—I don't know how to explain it—that you write novels. See, Teresina, this gentleman and I are writing a book together, all about a lady who married a silly husband—would you like to hear about it?"

Stroking the thin white face, with the wide forget-me-not eyes, of the pretty, thin little blonde, Lady Tal left Marion, to his extreme discomfort, seated on the edge of a straw chair by the side of the bed, a bag of oranges on his knees and absolutely no ideas in his head.

"She is so good," remarked the little girl, opening and shutting a little fan which Lady Tal had just given her, "and so beautiful. Is she your sister? She told me she had a brother whom she was very fond of, but I thought he was dead. She's like an angel in Paradise."

"Precisely, precisely," answered Marion, thinking at the same time what an uncommonly uncomfortable place Paradise must, in that case, be. All this was not at all what he had imagined when he had occasionally written about young ladies consoling the sick; this businesslike, bouncing, cheerful shake-up-your-pillows and shake-up-your-soul mode of proceeding.

Lady Tal, he decided within himself, had emphatically no soul; all he had just witnessed, proved it.

"Why do you do it?" he suddenly asked, as they emerged from the hospital cloisters. He knew quite well: merely because she was so abominably active.

"I don't know. I like ill folk. I'm always so disgustingly well myself; and you see with my poor brother, I'd got accustomed to ill folk, so I suppose I can't do without. I should like to settle in England—if it weren't for all those hateful relations of mine and of my husband's—and go and live in the East End and look after sick creatures. At least I think I should; but I know I shouldn't."

"Why not?" asked Marion.

"Why? Oh, well, it's making oneself conspicuous, you know, and all that. One hates to be thought eccentric, of course. And then, if I went to England, of course I should have to go into society, otherwise people would go and say that I was out of it and had been up to something or other. And if I went into society, that would mean doing simply nothing else, not even the little I do here. You see I'm not an independent woman; all my husband's relations are perpetually ready to pull me to pieces on account of his money! There's nothing they're not prepared to invent about me. I'm too poor and too expensive to do without it, and as long as I take his money, I must see to no one being able to say anything that would have annoyed him—see?"

"I see," answered Marion.

At that moment Lady Atalanta perceived a gondola turning a corner, and in it the young millionaire whom she had chaffed about his sideboard.

"Hi, hi! Mr. Clarence!" she cried, waving her umbrella. "Will you take me to that curiosity-dealer's this afternoon?"

Marion looked at her, standing there on the little wharf, waving her red umbrella and shouting to the gondola; her magnificent rather wooden figure more impeccably magnificent, uninteresting in her mannish flannel garments, her handsome pink and white face, as she smiled that inexpressive smile with all the pearl-like little teeth, more than ever like a big mask——;

"No soul, decidedly no soul," said the novelist to himself. And he reflected that women without souls were vaguely odious.

VII.

"I have been wondering of late why I liked you?" said Lady Tal one morning at lunch, addressing the remark to Marion, and cut short in her speech by a burst of laughter from that odious tomboy of a cousin of hers (how could she endure that girl? Marion reflected) who exclaimed, with an affectation of milkmaid archness:

"Oh, Tal! how *can* you be so rude to the *gentleman*? You oughtn't to say to people you wonder why you like them. Ought she, Mr. Marion?"

Marion was silent. He felt a weak worm for disliking this big blond girl with the atrocious manners, who insisted on pronouncing his name *Mary Anne*, with unfailing relish of the joke. Lady Tal did not heed the interruption, but repeated pensively, leaning her handsome cleft chin on her hand, and hacking at a peach with her knife: "I have been wondering why I like you, Mr. Marion (I usedn't to, but made up to you for *Christina's* benefit), because you are not a bit like poor Gerald. But I've found out now and I'm pleased. There's nothing so pleasant in this world as finding out *why* one thinks or does things, is there? Indeed it's the only pleasant thing, besides riding in the Campagna and drinking iced water on a hot day. The reason I like you is because you have seen a lot of the world and of people, and still take nice views of them. The people one meets always think to show their cleverness by explaining everything by nasty little motives; and you don't. It's nice of you, and it's clever. It's cleverer than your books even, you know."

In making this remark (and she made it with an aristocratic indifference to being personal) Lady Atalanta had most certainly hit the right nail on the head. That gift, a rare one, of seeing the simple, wholesome, and even comparatively noble, side of things; of being, although a pessimist, no misanthrope, was the most remarkable characteristic of Jervase Marion; it was the one which made him, for all his old bachelor ways and his shrinking from close personal contact, a man and a manly man, giving this analytical and nervous person a certain calmness and gentleness and strength.

But Lady Tal's remark, although in the main singularly correct, smote him like a rod. For it so happened that for once in his life Marion had not been looking with impartial, serene, and unsuspecting eyes upon one of his fellow-sufferers in this melancholy world; and that one creature to whom he was not so good as he might be, was just Lady Tal.

He could not really have explained how it was. But there was the certainty, that while recognising in Lady Tal's conversation, in her novel, in the little she told him of her life, a great deal which was delicate, and even noble, wherewithal to make up a somewhat unusual and perhaps not very superficially attractive, but certainly an original and desirable personality, he had got into the habit of explaining whatever in her was obscure and contradictory by unworthy reasons; and even of making allowance for the possibility of all the seeming good points proving, some day, to be a delusion and a snare. Perhaps it depended upon the constant criticisms he was hearing on all sides of Lady Atalanta's character and conduct: the story of her mercenary marriage, the recital of the astounding want of feeling displayed upon the occasion of her brother's death, and that perpetual, and apparently too well founded suggestion that this young lady, who possessed fifteen thousand a year and apparently spent about two, must be feathering her nest and neatly evading the intentions of her late lamented. Moreover there was something vaguely disagreeable in the extraordinary absence of human emotion displayed in such portion of her biography as might be considered public property.

Marion, heaven knows, didn't like women who went in for *grande passion*; in fact passion, which he had neither experienced nor described, was distinctly repulsive to him. But, after all, Lady Tal was young, Lady Tal was beautiful, and Lady Tal had for years and years been a real and undoubted widow; and it was therefore distinctly inhuman on the part of Lady Tal to have met no temptations to part with her heart, and with her jointure. It was ugly; there was no doubt it was ugly. The world, after all, *has* a right to demand that a young lady of good birth and average education should have a heart. It was doubtless also, he said to himself, the fault of Lady Atalanta's physique, this suspicious attitude of his; nature had bestowed upon her a face like a mask, muscles which never flinched, nerves apparently hidden many inches deeper than most folk's: she was enigmatic, and a man has a right to pause before an enigma. Furthermore——;But Marion could not quite understand that furthermore.

He understood it a few days later. They had had the usual *séance* over *Christina* that morning; and now it was evening, and three or four people had dropped in at Lady Tal's after the usual stroll at Saint Mark's. Lady Tal had hired a small house, dignified with the title of Palazzina, on the Zattere. It was modern, and the æsthetic colony at Venice sneered at a woman with that amount of money inhabiting anything short of a palace. They themselves being mainly Americans, declared they couldn't feel like home in a dwelling which was not possessed of historical reminiscences. The point of Lady Tal's little place, as she called it, was that it possessed a garden; small indeed, but round which, as she remarked, one solitary female could walk. In this garden she and Marion were at this moment walking. The ground floor windows were open, and there issued from the drawing-room a sound of cups and saucers, of guitar strumming and laughter, above which rose the loud voice, the aristocratic kitchen-maid pronunciation of Lady Atalanta's tomboy cousin.

"Where's Tal? I declare if Tal hasn't gone off with Mary Anne! Poor Mary Anne! She's tellin' him all about *Christina*, you know; how she can't manage that row between Christina and Christina's mother-in-law, and the semicolons and all that. *Christina's* the novel, you know. You'll be expected to ask for *Christina* at your club, you know, when it comes out, Mr. Clarence. I've already written to all my cousins to get it from Mudie's——;"

Marion gave a little frown, as if his boot pinched him, as he walked on the gravel down there, among the dark bushes, the spectral little terra-cotta statues, with the rigging of the ships on the Giudecca canal black against the blue evening sky, with a vague, sweet, heady smell of *Olea fragrans* all round. Confound that girl! Why couldn't he take a stroll in a garden with a handsome woman of thirty without the company being informed that it was only on account of Lady Tal's novel. That novel, that position of literary adviser, of a kind of male daily governess, would make him ridiculous. Of course Lady Tal was continually making use of him, merely making use of him in her barefaced and brutal manner: of course she didn't care a hang about him except to help her with that novel: of course as soon as that novel was done with she would drop him. He knew all that, and it was natural. But he really didn't see the joke of being made conspicuous and grotesque before all Venice——;

"Shan't we go in, Lady Tal?" he said sharply, throwing away his cigarette. "Your other guests are doubtless sighing for your presence."

"And this guest here is not. Oh dear, no; there's Gertrude to look after them and see to their being happy; besides, I don't care whether they are. I want to speak to you. I can't understand your thinking that situation strained. I should have thought it the commonest thing in the world, I mean, gracious——; I can't understand your not understanding!"

Jervase Marion was in the humour when he considered Lady Tal a legitimate subject of study, and intellectual vivisection a praiseworthy employment. Such study implies, as a rule, a good deal of duplicity on the part of the observer; duplicity doubtless sanctified, like all the rest, by the high mission of prying into one's neighbour's soul.

"Well," answered Marion—he positively hated that good French Alabama name of his, since hearing it turned into Mary Anne—"of course one understands a woman avoiding, for many reasons, the temptation of one individual passion; but a woman who makes up her mind to avoid the temptation of all passion in the abstract, and what is more, acts consistently and persistently with this object in view, particularly when she has never experienced passion at all, when she has not even burnt the tips of her fingers once in her life——;; that does seem rather far fetched, you must admit."

Lady Tal was not silent for a moment, as he expected she would be. She did not seem to see the danger of having the secret of her life extracted out of her.

"I don't see why you should say so, merely because the person's a woman. I'm sure you must have met examples enough of men who, without ever having been in love, or in danger of being in love—poor little things—have gone through life with a resolute policy of never placing themselves in danger, of never so much as taking their heart out of their waistcoat pockets to look at it, lest it might suddenly be jerked out of their possession."

It was Marion who was silent. Had it not been dark, Lady Tal might have seen him wince and redden; and he might have seen Lady Tal smile a very odd but not disagreeable smile. And they fell to discussing the technicalities of that famous novel.

Marion outstayed for a moment or two the other guests. The facetious cousin was strumming in the next room, trying over a Venetian song which the naval captain had taught her. Marion was slowly taking a third cup of tea—he wondered why he should be taking so much tea, it was very bad for his nerves,—seated among the flowering shrubs, the bits of old brocade and embroidery, the various pieces of bric-à-brac which made the drawing-room of Lady Tal look, as all distinguished modern drawing-rooms should, like a cross between a flower show and a pawnbroker's, and as if the height of modern upholstery consisted in avoiding the use of needles and nails, and enabling the visitors to sit in a little heap of variegated rags. Lady Tal was arranging a lamp, which burned, or rather smoked, at this moment, surrounded by lace petticoats on a carved column.

"Ah," she suddenly said, "it's extraordinary how difficult it is to get oneself understood in this world. I'm thinking about *Christina*, you know. I never *do* expect any one to understand anything, as a matter of fact. But I thought that was probably because all my friends hitherto have been all frivolous poops who read only the Peerage and the sporting papers. I should have thought, now, that writing novels would have made you different. I suppose, after all, it's all a question of physical constitution and blood relationship—being able to understand other folk, I mean. If one's molecules aren't precisely the same and in the same place (don't be surprised, I've been reading Carpenter's 'Mental Physiology'), it's no good. It's certain that the only person in the world who has ever understood me one bit was Gerald."

Lady Tal's back was turned to Marion, her tall figure a mere dark mass against the light of the lamp, and the lit-up white wall behind.

"And still," suddenly remarked Marion, "you were not—not—*very* much attached to your brother, were you?"

The words were not out of Marion's mouth before he positively trembled at them. Good God! what had he allowed himself to say? But he had no time to think of his own words. Lady Tal had turned round, her eyes fell upon him. Her face was pale, very quiet; not angry, but disdainful. With one hand she continued to adjust the lamp.

"I see," she said coldly, "you have heard all about my extraordinary behaviour, or want of extraordinary behaviour. It appears I did surprise and shock my acquaintances very much by my proceedings after Gerald's death. I suppose it really is the right thing for a woman to go into hysterics and take to her bed and shut herself up for three months at least, when her only brother dies. I didn't think of that at the time; otherwise I should have conformed, of course. It's my policy always to conform, you know. I see now that I made a mistake, showed a want of *savoir-vivre*, and all that—I stupidly consulted my own preferences, and I happened to prefer keeping myself well in hand. I didn't seem to like people's sympathy; now the world, you know, has a right to give one its sympathies under certain circumstances, just as a foreign man has a right to leave his card when he's been introduced. Also, I knew that Gerald would have just hated my making myself a *motley to the view*—you mightn't think it, but we used to read Shakespeare's sonnets, he and I—and, you see, I cared for only one mortal thing in the world, to do what Gerald wanted. I never have cared for any other thing, really; after all, if I don't want to be conspicuous, it's because Gerald would have hated it— I never shall care for anything in the world besides that. All the rest's mere unreality. One thinks one's alive, but one isn't."

Lady Atalanta had left off fidgeting with the lamp. Her big blue eyes had all at once brightened with tears which did not fall; but as she spoke the last words, in a voice suddenly husky, she looked down at Marion with an odd smile, tearing a paper spill with her large, well-shaped fingers as she did so.

"Do you see?" she added, with that half-contemptuous smile, calmly mopping her eyes. "That's how it is, Mr. Marion."

A sudden light illuminated Marion's mind; a light, and with it something else, he knew not what, something akin to music, to perfume, beautiful, delightful, but solemn. He was aware of being moved, horribly grieved, but at the same moment intensely glad; he was on the point of saying he didn't know beforehand what, something which, however, would be all right, natural, like the things, suddenly improvised, which one says occasionally to children.

"My dear young lady——;"

But the words did not pass Marion's lips. He remembered suddenly by what means and in what spirit he had elicited this unexpected burst of feeling on the part of Lady Tal. He could not let her go on, he could not take advantage of her; he had not the courage to say: "Lady Tal, I am a miserable cad who was prying into your feelings; I'm not fit to be spoken to!" And with the intolerable shame at his own caddishness came that old shrinking from any sort of spiritual contact with others.

"Quite so, quite so," he merely answered, looking at his boots and moving that ring of his mother's up and down his watch chain. "I quite understand. And as a matter of fact you are quite correct in your remark about our not being always alive. Or rather we *are* usually alive, when we are living our humdrum little natural existence, full of nothing at all; and during the moments when we do really seem to be alive, to be feeling, living, we are not ourselves, but somebody else."

Marion had had no intention of making a cynical speech. He had been aware of having behaved like a cad to Lady Tal, and in consequence, had somehow informed Lady Tal he considered her as an impostor. He had reacted against that first overwhelming sense of pleasure at the discovery of the lady's much-questioned soul. Now he was prepared to tell her that she had none.

"Yes," answered Lady Tal, lighting a cigarette over the high lamp, "that's just it. I shall borrow that remark and put it into *Christina*. You may use up any remark of mine, in return, you know."

She stuck out her under lip with that ugly little cynical movement which was not even her own property, but borrowed from women more trivial than herself like the way of carrying the elbows, and the pronunciation of certain words: a mark of caste, as a blue triangle on one's chin or a yellow butterfly on one's forehead might be, and not more graceful or engaging.

"One thinks one has a soul sometimes," she mused. "It isn't true. It would prevent one's clothes fitting, wouldn't it? One really acts in this way or that because *it's better form*. You see here on the Continent it's good form to tear one's hair and roll on the floor, and to pretend to have a soul; we've got beyond that, as we've got beyond women trying to seem to know about art and literature. Here they do, and make idiots of themselves. Just now you thought I'd got a soul, didn't you, Mr. Marion? You've been wondering all along whether I had one. For a minute I managed to make you believe it—it was rather mean of me, wasn't it? I haven't got one. I'm a great deal too well-bred."

There was a little soreness under all this banter; but how could she banter? Marion felt he detested the woman, as she put out her elbow and extended a stiff handsome hand, and said:

"Remember poor old *Christina* to-morrow morning, there's a kind man," with that little smile of close eyes and close lips. He detested her just in proportion as he had liked her half an hour ago. Remembering that little gush of feeling of his own, he thought her a base creature, as he walked across the little moonlit square with the well in the middle and the tall white houses all round.

Jervase Marion, the next morning, woke up with the consciousness of having been very unfair to Lady Tal, and, what was worse, very unfair to himself. It was one of the drawbacks of friendship (for, after all, this was a kind of friendship) that he occasionally caught himself saying things quite different from his thoughts and feelings, masquerading towards people in a manner distinctly humiliating to his self-respect. Marion had a desire to be simple and truthful; but somehow it was difficult to be simple and truthful as soon as other folk came into play; it was difficult and disagreeable to show one's real self; that was another reason for living solitary on a top flat at Westminster, and descending therefrom in the body, but not in the spirit, to move about among mere acquaintances, disembodied things, with whom there was no fear of real contact. On this occasion he had let himself come in contact with a fellow-creature; and behold, as a result, he had not only behaved more or less like a cad, but he had done that odious thing of pretending to feel differently from how he really did.

From how he had really felt at the moment, be it well understood. Of course Marion, in his capacity of modern analytical novelist, was perfectly well aware that feelings are mere momentary matters; and that the feeling which had possessed him the previous evening, and still possessed him at the present moment, would not last. The feeling, he admitted to himself (it is much easier to admit such things to one's self, when one makes the proviso that it's all a mere passing phase, one's eternal immutable self, looking on placidly at one's momentary changing self), the feeling in question was vaguely admiring and pathetic, as regarded Lady Tal. He even confessed to himself that there entered into it a slight dose of poetry. This big, correct young woman, with the beautiful inexpressive face and the ugly inexpressive manners, carrying through life a rather exotic little romance which no one must suspect, possessed a charm for the imagination, a decided value. Excluded for some reason (Marion blurred out his knowledge that the reasons were the late Walkenshaw's thousands) from the field for emotions and interests which handsome, big young women have a right to, and transferring them all to a nice crippled brother, who had of course not been half as nice as she imagined, living a conventional life, with a religion of love and fidelity secreted within it, this well-born and well-dressed Countess Olivia of modern days, had appealed very strongly to a certain carefully guarded tenderness and chivalry in Marion's nature; he saw her, as she had stood arranging that lamp, with those unexpected tears brimming in her eyes.

Decidedly. Only that, of course, wasn't the way to treat it. There was nothing at all artistic in that, nothing modern. And Marion was essentially modern in his novels. Lady Tal, doing the Lady Olivia, with a dead brother in the background, sundry dukes in the middle distance, and no enchanting page (people seemed unanimous in agreeing that Lady Tal had never been in love) perceptible anywhere; all that was pretty, but it wasn't the right thing. Jervase Marion thought Lady Tal painfully conventional (although of course her conventionality gave all the value to her romantic quality) because she slightly dropped her final *g*'s, and visibly stuck out her elbows, and resolutely refused to display emotion of any kind. Marion himself was firmly wedded to various modes of looking at human concerns, which corresponded, in the realm of novel-writing, to these same modern conventionalities of Lady Atalanta's. The point of it, evidently, must be that the Lady of his novel would have lived for years under the influence of an invalid friend (the brother should be turned into a woman with a mortal malady, and a bad husband, something in the way of Emma and Tony in "Diana of the Crossways," of intellectual and moral quality immensely superior to her own); then, of course, after the death of the Princess of Trasimeno (she being the late Gerald Burne), Lady Tal (Marion couldn't fix on a name for her) would gradually be sucked back into frivolous and futile and heartless society; the *hic* of the whole story being the slow ebbing of that noble influence, the daily encroachments of the baser sides of Lady Tal's own nature, and of the base side of the world. She would have a chance, say by marrying a comparatively poor man, of securing herself from that rising tide of worldly futility and meanness; the reader must think that she really was going to love the man, to choose him. Or rather, it would be more modern and artistic, less romantic, if the intelligent reader were made to foresee the dismal necessity of Lady Tal's final absorption into moral and intellectual nothingness. Yes—the sort of thing she would live for, a round of monotonous dissipation, which couldn't amuse her; of expenditure merely for the sake of expenditure, of conventionality merely for the sake of conventionality;—and the sham, clever, demoralised women, with their various semi-imaginary grievances against the world, their husbands and children, their feeble self-conscious hankerings after mesmerism, spiritualism, Buddhism, and the other forms of intellectual adulteration——;he saw it all. Marion threw his cigar into the canal, and nursed his leg tighter, as he sat all alone in his gondola, and looked up at the bay trees and oleanders, the yellow straw blinds of Lady Tal's little house on the Zattere.

It would make a capital novel. Marion's mind began to be inundated with details: all those conversations about Lady Tal rushed back into it, her conventionality, perceptible even to others, her disagreeable parsimoniousness, visibly feathering her nest with the late Walkenshaw's money, while quite unable to screw up her courage to deliberately forego it, that odd double-graspingness of nature.

That was evidently the final degradation. It would be awfully plucky to put it in, after showing what the woman had been and might have been; after showing her coquettings with better things (the writing of that novel, for instance, for which he must find an equivalent). It would be plucky, modern, artistic, to face the excessive sordidness of this ending. And still—and still——;Marion felt a feeble repugnance to putting it in; it seemed too horrid. And at the same moment, there arose in him that vague, disquieting sense of being a cad, which had distressed him that evening. To suspect a woman of all that——;and yet, Marion answered himself with a certain savageness, he knew it to be the case.

VIII.

They had separated from the rest of the picnickers, and were walking up and down that little orchard or field—rows of brown maize distaffs and tangles of reddening half trodden-down maize leaves, and patches of tall grass powdered with hemlock under the now rather battered vine garlands, the pomegranate branches weighed down by their vermilion fruit, the peach branches making a Japanese pattern of narrow crimson leaves against the blue sky—that odd cultivated corner in the God-forsaken little marsh island, given up to sea-gulls and picnickers, of Torcello.

"Poor little Clarence," mused Lady Tal, alluding to the rather feeble-minded young millionaire, who had brought them there, five gondolas full of women in lilac and pink and straw-coloured frocks, and men in white coats, three guitars, a banjo, and two mandolins, and the corresponding proportion of table linen, knives and forks, pies, bottles, and sweetmeats with crinkled papers round them. "Poor little Clarence, he isn't a bad little thing, is he? He wouldn't be bad to a woman who married him, would he?"

"He would adore her," answered Jervase Marion, walking up and down that orchard by Lady Tal's side. "He would give her everything the heart of woman could desire; carriages, horses, and diamonds, and frocks from Worth, and portraits by Lenbach and Sargent, and bric-à-brac, and—ever so much money for charities, hospitals, that sort of thing——;and——;and complete leisure and freedom and opportunities for enjoying the company of men not quite so well off as himself."

Marion stopped short, his hands thrust in his pockets, and with that frown which made people think that his boots pinched. He was looking down at his boots at this moment, though he was really thinking of that famous novel, his, not Lady Tal's; so Lady Tal may have perhaps thought it was the boots that made him frown, and speak in a short, cross little way. Apparently she thought so, for she took no notice of his looks, his intonation, or his speech.

"Yes," she continued musing, striking the ground with her umbrella, "he's a good little thing. It's good to bring us all to Torcello, with all that food and those guitars, and banjos and things, particularly as we none of us throw a word at him in return. And he seems so pleased. It shows a very amiable, self-effacing disposition, and that's, after all, the chief thing in marriage. But, Lord! how dreary it would be to see that man at breakfast, and lunch, and dinner! or if one didn't, merely to know that there he must be, having breakfast, lunch and dinner somewhere—for I suppose he would have to have them—that man existing somewhere on the face of the globe, and speaking of one as 'my wife.' Fancy knowing the creature was always smiling, whatever one did, and never more jealous than my umbrella. Wouldn't it feel like being one of the fish in that tank we saw? Wouldn't living with the Bishop—is he a bishop?—of Torcello, in that musty little house with all the lichen stains and mosquito nests, and nothing but Attila's throne to call upon—be fun compared with that? Yes, I suppose it's wise to marry Clarence. I suppose I shall do right in making him marry my cousin. You know"—she added, speaking all these words slowly—"I could make him marry anybody, because he wants to marry me."

Marion gave a little start as Lady Tal had slowly pronounced those two words, "my cousin." Lady Tal noticed it.

"You thought I had contemplated having Clarence myself?" she said, looking at the novelist with a whimsical, amused look. "Well, so I have. I have contemplated a great many things, and not had the courage to do them. I've contemplated going off to Germany, and studying nursing; and going off to France, and studying painting; I've contemplated turning Catholic, and going into a convent. I've contemplated—well—I'm contemplating at present— becoming a *great* novelist, as you know. I've contemplated marrying poor men, and becoming their amateur charwoman; and I've contemplated marrying rich men, and becoming—well, whatever a penniless woman does become when she marries a rich man; but I've done that once before, and once is enough of any experience in life, at least for a person of philosophic cast of mind, don't you think? I confess I have been contemplating the possibility of marrying Clarence, though I don't see my way to it. You see, it's not exactly a pleasant position to be a widow and not to be one, as I am, in a certain sense. Also, I'm bored with living on my poor husband's money, particularly as I know he wished me to find it as inconvenient as possible to do so. I'm bored with keeping the capital from that wretched boy and his mother, who would get it all as soon as I was safely married again. That's it. As a matter of fact I'm bored with all life, as I daresay most people are; but to marry this particular Clarence, or any other Clarence that may be disporting himself about, wouldn't somehow diminish the boringness of things. Do you see?"

"I see," answered Marion. Good Heavens, what a thing it is to be a psychological novelist! and how exactly he had guessed at the reality of Lady Atalanta's character and situation. He would scarcely venture to write that novel of his; he might as well call it *Lady Tal* at once. It was doubtless this discovery which made him grow suddenly very red and feel an intolerable desire to say he knew not what.

They continued walking up and down that little orchard, the brown maize leaves all around, the bright green and vermilion enamel of the pomegranate trees, the Japanese pattern, red and yellow, of the peach branches, against the blue sky above.

"My dear Lady Tal," began Marion, "my dear young lady, will you allow—an elderly student of human nature to say—how—I fear it must seem very impertinent—how thoroughly—taking your whole situation as if it were that of a third person—he understanding its difficulties—and, taking the situation no longer quite as that of a third person, how earnestly he hopes that——;"

Marion was going to say "you will not derogate from the real nobility of your nature." But only a fool could say such a thing; besides, of course, Lady Tal *must* derogate. So he finished off:

"That events will bring some day a perfectly satisfactory, though perhaps unforeseen, conclusion for you."

Lady Tal was paying no attention. She plucked one of the long withered peach leaves, delicate, and red, and transparent, like a Chinese visiting card, and began to pull it through her fingers.

"You see," she said, "of the income my husband left me, I've been taking only as much as seemed necessary—about two thousand a year. I mean necessary that people shouldn't see that I'm doing this sort of thing; because, after all, I suppose a woman could live on less, though I am an expensive woman.—The rest, of course, I've been letting accumulate for the heir; I couldn't give it him, for that would have been going against my husband's will. But it's rather boring to feel one's keeping that boy,—such a nasty young brute as he is—and his horrid mother out of all that money, merely by being there. It's rather humiliating, but it would be more humiliating to marry another man for his money. And I don't suppose a poor man would have me; and perhaps I wouldn't have a poor man. Now, suppose I were the heroine of your novel—you know you *are* writing a novel about me, that's what makes you so patient with me and *Christina*, you're just walking round, and looking at me——;"

"Oh, my dear Lady Tal—how—how can you think such a thing!" gobbled out Marion indignantly. And really, at the moment of speaking, he did feel a perfectly unprofessional interest in this young lady, and was considerably aggrieved at this accusation.

"Aren't you? Well, I thought you were. You see I have novel on the brain. Well, just suppose you *were* writing that novel, with me for a heroine, what would you advise me? One has got accustomed to having certain things—a certain amount of clothes, and bric-à-brac and horses, and so forth, and to consider them necessary. And yet, I think if one were to lose them all to-morrow, it wouldn't make much difference. One would merely say: 'Dear me, what's become of it all?' And yet I suppose one does require them—other people have them, so I suppose it's right one should have them also. Other people like to come to Torcello in five gondolas with three guitars, a banjo, and lunch, and to spend two hours feeding and littering the grass with paper bags; so I suppose one ought to like it too. If it's right, I like it. I always conform, you know; only it's rather dull work, don't you think, considered as an interest in life? Everything is dull work, for the matter of that, except dear old *Christina*. What do you think one might do to make things a little less dull? But perhaps everything is equally dull——;"

Lady Tal raised one of those delicately-pencilled, immensely arched eyebrows of hers, with a sceptical little sigh, and looked in front of her, where they were standing.

Before them rose the feathery brown and lilac of the little marsh at the end of the orchard, long seeding reeds, sere grasses, sea lavender, and Michaelmas daisy; and above that delicate bloom, on an unseen strip of lagoon, moved a big yellow and brown sail, slowly flapping against the blue sky. From the orchard behind, rose at intervals the whirr of a belated cicala; they heard the dry maize leaves crack beneath their feet.

"It's all very lovely," remarked Lady Tal pensively; "but it doesn't somehow fit in properly. It's silly for people like me to come to such a place. As a rule, since Gerald's death, I only go for walks in civilized places: they're more in harmony with my frocks."

Jervase Marion did not answer. He leaned against the bole of a peach tree, looking out at the lilac and brown sea marsh and the yellow sail, seeing them with that merely physical intentness which accompanies great mental preoccupation. He was greatly moved. He was aware of a fearful responsibility. Yet neither the emotion nor the responsibility made him wretched, as he always fancied that all emotion or responsibility must.

He seemed suddenly to be in this young woman's place, to feel the already begun, and rapid increasing withering-up of this woman's soul, the dropping away from it of all real, honest, vital interests. She seemed to him in horrible danger, the danger of something like death. And there was but one salvation: to give up that money, to make herself free——;Yes, yes, there was nothing for it but that. Lady Tal, who usually struck him as so oppressively grown up, powerful, able to cope with everything, affected him at this moment as a something very young, helpless, almost childish; he understood so well that during all those years this big woman in her stiff clothes, with her inexpressive face, had been a mere child in the hands of her brother, that she had never thought, or acted, or felt for herself; that she had not lived.

Give up that money; give up that money; marry some nice young fellow who will care for you; become the mother of a lot of nice little children——;The words went on and on in Marion's mind, close to his lips; but they could not cross them. He almost saw those children of hers, the cut of their pinafores and sailor clothes, the bend of their blond and pink necks; and that nice young husband, blond of course, tall of course, with vague, regular features, a little dull perhaps, but awfully good. It was so obvious, so right. At the same time it seemed rather tame; and Marion, he didn't know why, while perceiving its extreme rightness and delightfulness, couldn't help wincing a little bit at the prospect——;

Lady Tal must have been engaged simultaneously in some similar contemplation, for she suddenly turned round, and said:

"But after all, anything else might perhaps be just as boring as all this. And fancy having given up that money all for nothing; one would feel such a fool. On the whole, my one interest in life is evidently destined to be *Christina*, and the solution of all my doubts will be the appearance of the 'New George Eliot of fashionable life'; don't you think that sounds like the heading in one of your American papers, the Buffalo *Independent*, or Milwaukee *Republican*?"

Marion gave a little mental start.

"Just so, just so," he answered hurriedly: "I think it would be a fatal thing— a very fatal thing for you to—well—to do anything rash, my dear Lady Tal. After all, we must remember that there is such a thing as habit; a woman accustomed to the life you lead, although I don't deny it may sometimes seem dull, would be committing a mistake, in my opinion a great mistake, in depriving herself, for however excellent reasons, of her fortune. Life is dull, but, on the whole, the life we happen to live is usually the one which suits us best. My own life, for instance, strikes me at moments, I must confess, as a trifle dull. Yet I should be most unwise to change it, most unwise. I think you are quite right in supposing that novel-writing, if you persevere in it, will afford you a—very—well—a—considerable interest in life."

Lady Tal yawned under her parasol.

"Don't you think it's time for us to go back to the rest of our rabble?" she asked. "It must be quite three-quarters of an hour since we finished lunch, so I suppose it's time for tea, or food of some sort. Have you ever reflected, Mr. Marion, how little there would be in picnics, and in life in general, if one couldn't eat a fresh meal every three-quarters of an hour?"

IX.

Few things, of the many contradictory things of this world, are more mysterious than the occasional certainty of sceptical men. Marion was one of the most sceptical of sceptical novelists; the instinct that nothing really depended upon its supposed or official cause, that nothing ever produced its supposed or official effect, that all things were always infinitely more important or unimportant than represented, that nothing is much use to anything, and the world a mystery and a muddle; this instinct, so natural to the psychologist, regularly honeycombed his existence, making it into a mere shifting sand, quite unfit to carry the human weight. Yet at this particular moment, Marion firmly believed that if only Lady Atalanta could be turned into a tolerable novelist, the whole problem of Lady Atalanta's existence would be satisfactorily solved, if only she could be taught construction, style, punctuation, and a few other items; if only one could get into her head the difference between a well-written thing, and an ill-written thing, then, considering her undoubted talent——;for Marion's opinion of Lady Tal's talent had somehow increased with a bound. Why he should think *Christina* a more remarkable performance now that he had been tinkering at it for six weeks, it is difficult to perceive. He seemed certainly to see much more in it. Through that extraordinary difficulty of expression, he now felt the shape of a personality, a personality contradictory, enigmatical, not sure of itself, groping, as it were, to the light. *Christina* was evidently the real Lady Tal, struggling through that overlaying of habits and prejudices which constituted the false one.

So, *Christina* could not be given too much care; and certainly no novel was ever given more, both by its author and by its critic. There was not a chapter, and scarcely a paragraph, which had not been dissected by Marion and re-written by Lady Tal; the critical insight of the one being outdone only by the scribbling energy of the other. And now, it would soon be finished. There was only that piece about Christina's reconciliation with her sister-in-law to get into shape. Somehow or other the particular piece seemed intolerably difficult to do; the more Lady Tal worked at it, the worse it grew; the more Marion expounded his views on the subject, the less did she seem able to grasp them.

They were seated on each side of the big deal table, which, for the better development of *Christina*, Lady Tal had installed in her drawing-room, and which at this moment presented a lamentable confusion of foolscap, of mutilated pages, of slips for gumming on, of gum-pots, and scissors. The scissors, however, were at present hidden from view, and Lady Tal, stooping over the litter, was busily engaged looking for them.

"Confound those beastly old scissors!" she exclaimed, shaking a heap of MS. with considerable violence.

Marion, on his side, gave a feeble stir to the mass of paper, and said, rather sadly: "Are you sure you left them on this table?"

He felt that something was going wrong. Lady Tal had been unusually restive about the alterations he wanted her to make.

"You are slanging those poor scissors because you are out of patience with things in general, Lady Tal."

She raised her head, and leaning both her long, well-shaped hands on the table, looked full at Marion:

"Not with things in general, but with things in particular. With *Christina*, in the first place; and then with myself; and then with you, Mr. Marion."

"With me?" answered Marion, forcing out a smile of pseudo-surprise. He had felt all along that she was irritated with him this morning.

"With you"—went on the lady, continuing to rummage for the scissors—"with you, because I don't think you've been quite fair. It isn't fair to put it into an unfortunate creature's head that she is an incipient George Eliot, when you know that if she were to slave till doomsday, she couldn't produce a novel fit for the *Family Herald*. It's very ungrateful of me to complain, but you see it is rather hard lines upon me. You can do all this sort of thing as easy as winking, and you imagine that everyone else must. You put all your own ideas into poor *Christina*, and you just expect me to be able to carry them out, and when I make a hideous hash, you're not satisfied. You think of that novel just as if it were you writing it—you know you do. Well, then, when a woman discovers at last that she can't make the beastly thing any better; that she's been made to hope too much, and that too much is asked of her, you understand it's rather irritating. I am sick of re-writing that thing, sick of every creature in it."

And Lady Tal gave an angry toss to the sheets of manuscript with the long pair of dressmaker's scissors, which she had finally unburied. Marion felt a little pang. The pang of a clever man who discovers himself to be perpetrating a stupidity. He frowned that little frown of the tight boots.

Quite true. He saw, all of a sudden, that he really had been over-estimating Lady Tal's literary powers. It appeared to him monstrous. The thought made him redden. To what unjustifiable lengths had his interest in the novel—the novel in the abstract, anybody's novel; and (he confessed to himself) the interest in one novel in particular, his own, the one in which Lady Tal should figure—led him away! Perceiving himself violently to be in the wrong, he proceeded to assume the manner, as is the case with most of us under similar circumstances (perhaps from a natural instinct of balancing matters) of a person conscious of being in the right.

"I think," he said, dryly, "that you have rather overdone this novel, Lady Tal—worked at it too much, talked of it too much too, sickened yourself with it."

"—And sickened others," put in Lady Atalanta gloomily.

"No, no, no—not others—only yourself, my dear young lady," said Marion paternally, in a way which clearly meant that she had expressed the complete truth, being a rude woman, but that he, being a polite man, could never admit it. As a matter of fact, Marion was not in the least sick of *Christina*, quite the reverse.

"You see," he went on, playing with the elastic band of one of the packets of MS., "you can't be expected to know these things. But no professed novelist—no one of any experience—no one, allow me to say so, except a young lady, could possibly have taken such an overdose of novel-writing as you have. Why, you have done in six weeks what ought to have taken six months! The result, naturally, is that you have lost all sense of proportion and quality; you really can't see your novel any longer, that's why you feel depressed about it."

Lady Tal was not at all mollified.

"That wasn't a reason for making me believe I was going to be George Eliot and Ouida rolled into one, with the best qualities of Goethe and Dean Swift into the bargain," she exclaimed.

Marion frowned, but this time internally. He really had encouraged Lady Tal quite unjustifiably. He doubted, suddenly, whether she would ever get a publisher; therefore he smiled, and remarked gently:

"Well, but—in matters of belief, there are two parties, Lady Tal. Don't you think you may be partly responsible for this—this little misapprehension?"

Lady Tal did not answer. The insolence of the Ossian was roused. She merely looked at Marion from head to foot; and the look was ineffably scornful. It seemed to say: "This is what comes of a woman like me associating with Americans and novelists."

"I've not lost patience," she said after a moment; "don't think that. When I make up my mind to a thing I just do it. So I shall finish *Christina*, and print her, and publish her, and dedicate her to you. Only, catch me ever writing another novel again!—and"—she added, smiling with her closed teeth as she extended a somewhat stiff hand to Marion—"catch you reading another novel of mine again either, now that you've made all the necessary studies of me for *your* novel!"

Marion smiled politely. But he ran downstairs, and through the narrow little paved lane to the ferry at San Vio with a bent head.

He had been a fool, a fool, he repeated to himself. Not, as he had thought before, by exposing Lady Tal to disappointment and humiliation, but by exposing himself.

Yes, he understood it all. He understood it when, scarcely out of Lady Tal's presence, he caught himself, in the garden, looking up at her windows, half expecting to see her, to hear some rather rough joke thrown at him as a greeting, just to show she was sorry——; He understood it still better, when, every time the waiter knocked in the course of the day, he experienced a faint expectation that it might be a note from Lady Tal, a line to say: "I was as cross as two sticks, this morning, wasn't I?" or merely: "don't forget to come to-morrow."

He understood. He and the novel, both chucked aside impatiently by this selfish, capricious, imperious young aristocrat: the two things identified, and both now rejected as unworthy of taking up more of her august attention! Marion felt the insult to the novel—her novel—almost more than to himself. After all, how could Lady Tal see the difference between him and the various mashers of her acquaintance, perceive that he was the salt of the earth? She had not wherewithal to perceive it. But that she should not perceive the dignity of her own work, how infinitely finer that novel was than herself, how it represented all her own best possibilities; that she should be ungrateful for the sensitiveness with which he had discovered its merit, *her* merits, in the midst of that confusion of illiterate fashionable rubbish——;

And when that evening, having his coffee at St. Mark's, he saw Lady Tal's stately figure, her white dress, amongst the promenaders in the moonlight, a rabble of young men and women at her heels, it struck him suddenly that something was over. He thought that, if Lady Tal came to London next spring, he would not call upon her unless sent for; and he was sure she would not send for him, for as to *Christina*, *Christina* would never get as far as the proof-sheets; and unless *Christina* re-appeared on the surface, he also would remain at the bottom.

Marion got up from his table, and leaving the brightly illuminated square and the crowd of summer-like promenaders, he went out on to the Riva, and walked slowly towards the arsenal. The contrast was striking. Out here it looked already like winter. There were no chairs in front of the cafés, there were scarcely any gondola-lights at the mooring places. The passers-by went along quickly, the end of their cloak over their shoulder. And from the water, which swished against the marble landings, came a rough, rainy wind. It was dark, and there were unseen puddles along the pavement.

This was the result of abandoning, for however little, one's principles. He had broken through his convictions by accepting to read a young lady's MS. novel. It did not seem a very serious mistake. But through that chink, what disorderly powers had now entered his well-arranged existence!

What the deuce did he want with the friendship of a Lady Tal? He had long made up his mind to permit himself only such friendship as could not possibly involve any feeling, as could not distress or ruffle him by such incidents as illness, death, fickleness, ingratitude. The philosophy of happiness, of that right balance of activities necessary for the dispassionate student of mankind, consisted in never having anything that one could miss, in never wanting anything. Had he not long ago made up his mind to live contemplative only of external types, if not on a column like Simon Stylites, at least in its meaner modern equivalent, a top flat at Westminster?

Marion felt depressed, ashamed of his depression, enraged at his shame; and generally intolerably mortified at feeling anything at all, and still more, in consequence, at feeling all this much.

As he wandered up and down one of the stretches of the Riva, the boisterous wind making masts and sails creak, and his cigar-smoke fly wildly about, he began, however, to take a little comfort. All this, after all, was so much experience; and experience was necessary for the comprehension of mankind. It was preferable, as a rule, to use up other people's experience; to look down, from that top flat at Westminster, upon grief and worry and rage *in corpore vili*, at a good five storeys below one. But, on reflection, it was doubtless necessary occasionally to get impressions a little nearer; the very recognition of feeling in others presupposed a certain minimum of emotional experience in oneself.

Marion had a sense of humour, a sense of dignity, and a corresponding aversion to being ridiculous. He disliked extremely having played the part of the middle-aged fool. But if ever he should require, for a future novel, a middle-aged fool, why, there he would be, ready to hand. And really, unless he had thus miserably broken through his rules of life, thus contemptibly taken an interest in a young lady six-foot high, the daughter of a bankrupt earl, with an inexpressive face and a sentimental novel, he would never, never have got to fathom, as he now fathomed, the character of the intelligent woman of the world, with aspirations ending in frivolity, and a heart entirely rusted over by insolence.

Ah, he *did* understand Lady Tal. He had gone up to his hotel; and shut his window with a bang, receiving a spout of rain in his face, as he made that reflection. Really, Lady Tal might be made into something first-rate.

He threw himself into an arm-chair and opened a volume of the correspondence of Flaubert.

X.

"I am glad to have made an end of *Christina*," remarked Lady Tal, when they were on Miss Vanderwerf's balcony together. *Christina* had been finished, cleaned up, folded, wrapped in brown paper, stringed, sealing-waxed and addressed to a publisher, a week almost ago. During the days separating this great event from this evening, the last of Lady Atalanta's stay in Venice, the two novelists had met but little. Lady Tal had had farewell visits to pay, farewell dinners and lunches to eat. So had Jervase Marion; for, two days after Lady Tal's return to her apartment near the Holy Apostles at Rome, he would be setting out for that dear, tidy, solitary flat at Westminster.

"I am glad to have made an end of *Christina*," remarked Lady Tal, "it had got to bore me fearfully."

Marion winced. He disliked this young woman's ingratitude and brutality. It was ill-bred and stupid; and of all things in the world, the novelist from Alabama detested ill-breeding and stupidity most. He was angry with himself for minding these qualities in Lady Tal. Had he not long made up his mind that she possessed them, *must* possess them?

There was a pause. The canal beneath them was quite dark, and the room behind quite light; it was November, and people no longer feared lamps on account of mosquitoes, any more than they went posting about in gondolas after illuminated singing boats. The company, also, was entirely collected within doors; the damp sea-wind, the necessity for shawls and overcoats, took away the Romeo and Juliet character from those little gothic balconies, formerly crowded with light frocks and white waistcoats.

The temperature precluded all notions of flirtation; one must intend business, or be bent upon catching cold, to venture outside.

"How changed it all is!" exclaimed Lady Tal, "and what a beastly place Venice does become in autumn. If I were a benevolent despot, I should forbid any rooms being let or hotels being opened beyond the 15th of October. I wonder why I didn't get my bags together and go earlier! I might have gone to Florence or Perugia for a fortnight, instead of banging straight back to

Rome. Oh, of course, it was all along of *Christina*! What were we talking about? Ah, yes, about how changed it all was. Do you remember the first evening we met here, a splendid moonlight, and ever so hot? When was it? Two months ago? Surely more. It seems years ago. I don't mean merely on account of the change of temperature, and leaving off cotton frocks and that: I mean we seem to have been friends so long. You will write to me sometimes, won't you, and send any of your friends to me? Palazzo Malaspini, Santi Apostoli (just opposite the French Embassy, you know), after five nearly always, in winter. I wonder," continued Lady Tal, musingly, leaning her tweed elbow on the damp balustrade, "whether we shall ever write another novel together; what do you think, Mr. Marion?"

Something seemed suddenly to give away inside Marion's soul. He saw, all at once, those big rooms, which he had often heard described (a woman of her means ought to be ashamed of such furniture, the Roumanian Princess had remarked), near the Holy Apostles at Rome: the red damask walls, the big palms and azaleas, with pieces of embroidery wrapped round the pots, the pastel of Lady Tal by Lenbach, the five hundred photographs dotted about, and fifteen hundred silver objects of indeterminable shape and art, and five dozen little screens all covered with odd bits of brocade—of course there was all that: and the door curtain raised, and the butler bowing in, and behind him the whitish yellowish curl, and pinky grey face of Clarence. And then he saw, but not more distinctly, his writing-table at Westminster, the etchings round his walls, the collection of empty easy-chairs, each easier and emptier, with its book-holding or leg-stretching apparatus, than its neighbor. He became aware of being old, remarkably old, of a paternal position towards this woman of thirty. He spoke in a paternal tone—

"No!" he answered, "I think not. I shall be too busy. I must write another novel myself."

"What will your novel be about?" asked Lady Tal, slowly, watching her cigarette cut down through the darkness into the waters below. "Tell me."

"My novel? What will my novel be about?" repeated Marion, absently. His mind was full of those red rooms at Rome, with the screens, and the palms, and odious tow-coloured head of Clarence. "Why, my novel will be the story of an old artist, a sculptor—I don't mean a man of the Renaissance, I mean old in years, elderly, going on fifty—who was silly enough to imagine it was all love of art which made him take a great deal of interest in a certain young lady and her paintings——;"

"You said he was a sculptor just now," remarked Lady Tal calmly.

"Of course I meant in her statues—modelling—what d'you call it——;"

"And then?" asked Lady Tal after a pause, looking down into the canal. "What happened?"

"What happened?" repeated Marion, and he heard his own voice with surprise, wondering how it could be his own, or how he could know it for his, so suddenly had it grown quick and husky and unsteady—"What happened? Why—that he made an awful old fool of himself. That's all."

"That's all!" mused Lady Tal. "Doesn't it seem rather lame? You don't seem to have got sufficient *dénouement*, do you? Why shouldn't we write that novel together? I'm sure I could help you to something more conclusive than that. Let me see. Well, suppose the lady were to answer: 'I am as poor as a rat, and I fear I'm rather expensive. But I *can* make my dresses myself if only I get one of those wicker dolls, I call them Theresa, you know; and I *might* learn to do my hair myself; and then I'm going to be a great painter—no, sculptor, I mean—and make pots of money; so suppose we get married.' Don't you think Mr. Marion, that would be more *modern* than your *dénouement?* You would have to find out what that painter—no, sculptor, I beg your pardon—would answer. Consider that both he and the lady are rather lonely, bored, and getting into the sere and yellow——; We ought to write that novel together, because I've given you the ending—and also because I really can't manage another all by myself, now that I've got accustomed to having my semicolons put in for me——;"

As Lady Atalanta spoke these words, a sudden downpour of rain drove her and Marion back into the drawing-room.

A WORLDLY WOMAN.

I.

"But why should you mind who buys your pots, so long as your pots are beautiful?" asked the girl.

"Because as things exist at present, art can minister only to the luxury of the rich, idle classes. The people, the people that works and requires to play, and requires something to tell it of happier things, gets no share in art. The people is too poor to possess beautiful things, and too brutish to care for them: the only amusement it can afford is getting drunk. And one wearies and sickens of merely adding one's grain of sand to the inequality and injustice of existing social conditions—don't you see, Miss Flodden?"

Leonard Greenleaf stopped short, his breathlessness mingling with the annoyance at having let himself be carried away by his ideas, and producing a vague sense of warm helplessness.

"Of course," he went on, taking up a big jar of yellow Hispano-Moorish lustre ware, and mechanically dusting it with the feather brush, "it's absurd to talk like that about such things as pots, and it's absurd to talk like that to you."

And raising his head he gave a furtive little glare at the girl, where she stood in a golden beam of dust and sunlight, which slanted through his workshop.

Miss Valentine Flodden—for such was the name on the family card which she had sent in together with that of Messrs. Boyce—made rather a delightful picture in that yellow halo: the green light from under the plane trees filtering in through the door behind her, and gleams of crimson and glints of gold flickering, in the brown gloom wherever an enamel plate or pot was struck by a sunbeam, winnowed by the blind which flapped in the draught. Greenleaf knew by some dim, forgotten experience or unaccountable guess-work, that she was what was called, in the detestable jargon of a certain set, a pretty woman. He also recognised in her clothes—they were would-be manly, far more simple and practical than those of the girls he knew, yet telling of a life anything but practical and simple—that she belonged to that same set of persons; a fact apparent also in her movements, her words and accent, nay in the something indefinable in her manner which seemed to take things for granted. But he didn't care for her being beautiful. His feeling was solely of vague irritation at having let himself speak—he had quite unnecessarily told her he intended giving up the pottery next year—about the things which were his very life, to a stranger; a stranger who had come with a card to ask advice about her own amateur work, and from out of a world which was foreign and odious to him, the world of idleness and luxury. Also, he experienced slight shame at a certain silly, half-romantic pleasure at what was in reality the unconscious intrusion of a fashionable eccentric. This girl, who had been sent on from Boyce & Co.'s for information which they could not give, must evidently have thought she was coming to another shop, otherwise she would never have come all alone; she evidently took him for a shopman, otherwise she would not have staid so long nor spoken so freely. It was much better she should continue to regard him as a shopman; and indeed was it not his pride to have shaken off all class distinctions, and to have become a workingman like any other?

It was this thought which made him alter his tone and ask with grave politeness, "Is there any further point upon which I can have the pleasure of giving you any information?"

Miss Flodden did not answer this question. She stood contemplating the old warped oaken floor, on whose dust she was drawing a honeysuckle pattern with the end of her parasol.

"Why did you say that you ought not to speak about such things to—people, Mr. Greenleaf?" she asked. "Of course, one's a Philistine, and in outer darkness, but still——;"

She had raised her eyes full upon him. They were a strange light blue, darkening as she spoke, under very level brows, and she had an odd way of opening them out at one. Like that, with her delicate complexion, and a little vagueness about the mouth, she looked childish, appealing, and rather pathetic.

"All these things are very interesting," she added quickly; "at least they must be if one understands anything about them."

Greenleaf was sorry. He didn't know exactly why; but he felt vaguely as if he had been brutal. He had made her shut up—for he recognised that the second part of her speech was the reaction against his own; and that was brutal. He ought not to have let the conversation depart from the technicalities of pottery, as he had done by saying he intended giving it up, and then bursting into that socialistic rhapsody. It wasn't fair upon her.

By this time the reaction had completely set in with her. Her face had a totally different expression, indifferent, bored, a little insolent—the expression of her society and order.

"It's been very good of you," she said, looking vaguely round the room, with the shimmer of green leaves and the glint of enamel in its brown dustiness, "to tell me so many things, and to have given up so much of your time. I didn't know, you know, from Messrs. Boyce, that I was breaking in upon you at your work. I suppose they were so kind because of my father having a collection—they thought that I knew more about pottery than I do."

She stretched out her hand stiffly. Leonard Greenleaf did not know whether he ought to take it, because he guessed that she did not know whether she ought to offer it him. Also he felt awkward, and sorry to have shut her up.

"I should—be very happy to tell you anything more that I could, Miss Flodden," he said; "besides, the owners of Yetholme must be privileged people with us potters."

"If—if ever you be passing anywhere near Eaton Square—that's where I live with my aunt," she said, "won't you come in and have a cup of tea? Number 5; the number is on the card. But," she added suddenly, with a little laugh, which was that social stiffening once more, "perhaps you never do pass anywhere near tea-time; or you pass and don't come in. It would be a great waste of your time."

What had made her stiffen suddenly like that was a faint smile which had come into Greenleaf's face at the beginning of her invitation. He had understood, or thought he understood, that his visitor had grasped the fact of his being a sort of gentleman after all, and that she thought it necessary to express her recognition of the difference between him and any other member of the firm of Boyce & Co. by asking him to call.

"Of course you are a great deal too busy," she repeated. "Perhaps some day you will let me come to your studio again—some day next year—good-bye."

"Shall I call you a hansom?" he asked, wondering whether he had been rude.

"Thank you; I think I'll go by the Underground. You cross the big square, and then along the side of the British Museum, don't you? I made a note of the way as I came. Or else I'll get a 'bus in Tottenham Court Road."

She spoke the words *'bus* and *Underground*, he thought, with a little emphasis. She was determined to have her fill of eccentricity, now that she had gone in for pottery, and for running about all alone to strange places, and scoring out everything save her own name on the family card. At least so Greenleaf said to himself, as he watched the tall, slight young figure disappearing down the black Bloomsbury street, and among the green leaves and black stems of the Bloomsbury square. An unlikely apparition, oddly feminine in its spruce tailoring, in that sleepy part of the world, whence fashion had retreated long, long ago, with the last painted coach which had rumbled through the iron gates, and the last link which had been extinguished in the iron extinguishers of the rusty areas.

II.

Greenleaf had a great disbelief in his own intuitions; perhaps because he vibrated unusually to the touch of other folks' nature, and that the number and variety of his impressions sometimes made it difficult to come to a cut-and-dry conclusion. There was in him also a sensitiveness on the subject of his own beliefs and ideals which made him instinctively avoid contact with other folk, and avoid even knowing much about them. He often felt that in a way he was very unfit to be a Socialist and an agitator; for besides the absurd attraction that everything beautiful, distinguished, exotic, exercised upon him, and a corresponding repugnance to the coarse and sordid sights of the world, he knew himself to look at people in an excessively subjective way, never seeking spontaneously to understand what they themselves were trying to do and say, but analysing them merely from the series of impressions which he received. Just as his consciousness of being a born æsthete and aristocrat had pushed him into social questions and democratic views; so also his extreme conscientiousness occasionally made him attempt, rather abortively, to behave to others as he might wish to be behaved to himself, his imagination being taxed to the utmost by the inquiry as to what behaviour would be altruistic and just under the circumstances.

This preamble is necessary to explain various inconsistencies in our hero's conduct, and more particularly at this moment, the inconsistency of suddenly veering round in his suppositions about Miss Valentine Flodden. In his monotonous life of artistic work and social study—in those series of quiet days, as like one another as the rows of black Bloomsbury houses with their garlanded door-lintels and worn-out doorsteps, as the spear-heads of the railings, the spikes of blossom on the horse-chestnuts, and the little lions on the chain curbs round the British Museum—the weekly firing of his pottery kiln at Boyce's Works near Wandsworth, the weekly lecture to workingmen down at Whitechapel, the weekly reception in the sooty rooms of Faber, the Socialist poet and critic who had married the Socialist painter—all these were the landmarks of Greenleaf's existence, and landmarks of the magnitude of martello towers along a sea-shore. So that anything at all unexpected became, in his life of subversive thoughts and methodical activity, an incident and an adventure.

Thus it was that the visit of Miss Flodden, although he repeatedly noted its utter unimportance to himself and everyone else, became the theme of much idle meditation in the intervals of his work and study. He felt it as extraordinarily strange. And feeling it in this way, his conscientious good sense caused him to analyse it as sometimes almost unusually commonplace.

It was in consequence of repeatedly informing himself that after all nothing could be more natural than this visit, that he took the step which brought him once more into contact with the eccentricity of the adventure. For he repeated so often to himself how natural it was that a girl with a taste for art should care for pottery (particularly as her father owned the world-famous Yetholme collection), and caring for pottery should go for information to Messrs. Boyce's the decorators, and being referred by Boyce's to himself should come on, at once, and quite alone, to the studio of his unknown self; he identified Miss Flodden so completely with any one of the mature maidens who carried their peacock blue and sage green and amber beads, and interest in economics, archæology and so forth freely through his world, that he decided to give Miss Flodden the assistance which he would have proffered to one of the independent and studious spinsters of Bloomsbury and West Kensington. Accordingly he took a sheet of paper with "Boyce & Co., Decorators," stamped at the head of it, and wrote a note directed to Miss Valentine Flodden, Eaton Square, saying that as she would doubtless be interested in examining the Rhodian and Damascene pottery of the British Museum, which she had told him she knew very imperfectly, he ventured to enclose an introduction to the Head of the Department, whom she would find a most learned and amiable old gentleman; the fact of her connection with the famous Yetholme collection would, for the rest, be introduction enough in itself.

After posting the note and the enclosure, Leonard Greenleaf reflected, with some wonder and a little humiliation, that he had chosen a sheet of Boyce's business paper to write to Miss Flodden; while he had selected a sheet with the name of his old Oxford college for writing to the Head of the Department. But it was not childish contradictoriness after all; at least so he told himself. For old Colonel Hancock Dunstan (one never dropped the Colonel even in one's thoughts) had a weakness in favour of polite society and against new-fangled democracy, and liked Greenleaf exactly because he had better shaped hands and a better cut coat than other men who haunted the Museum. And as to Miss Flodden, why, it seemed more appropriate to keep things on the level of pottery and decoration, and therefore to have Boyce & Co. well to the fore.

Greenleaf had made up his mind that Fate would never again bring him face to face with Miss Flodden, and that he would certainly take no steps towards altering Fate's intentions. It was for this very reason that he had introduced the lady to his old friend of the Museum: for it is singular how introducing someone to somebody else keeps up the sense of the someone's presence; and how, occasionally, one insists upon such vicarious company. But, as stated already, he never dreamed, at least he thought he never dreamed, to see his eccentric young visitor again.

Such being the case, it might seem odd, had not his experience of human feelings destroyed all perception of oddity, that Greenleaf experienced no surprise when, obeying a peremptory scrawl from the former terror of Pashas and the present terror of scholars, he found himself one afternoon in Colonel Dunstan's solemn bachelor drawing-room, and in the presence once more of Miss Valentine Flodden.

Colonel Hancock Dunstan, who in his distant days had gone to Mecca disguised as a pilgrim, dug up Persian temples, slain uncivil Moslems with his own hand, and altogether constituted a minor Eastern question in his one boisterous self, had now settled down (a Government post having been created expressly to keep him quiet) into a life divided between furious archæological disputes and faithful service of the fair sex. He was at this moment promenading his shrunken person—which somehow straightened out into military vigour in the presence of young ladies—round a large table spread with innumerable cups of tea, plates of strawberries and dishes of bonbons. Of this he partook only in the spirit, offering it all, together with the service of a severe housekeeper and a black, barefooted Moor, for the consumption of his fair guests. The other guest, indeed, a gaunt and classic female archæologist, habited in peacock plush, was fair only in mind; and Colonel Dunstan, devoted as he was to all womankind, was wont to neglect such intellectual grace when in the presence of more obvious external beauty. Hence, at this moment, the poor archæological lady, accustomed to a shower of invitations to lunch, tea, dinner, and play-tickets from the gallant though terrible old man, was abandoned to the care of the housekeeper until she could be passed over to that of Greenleaf. And Colonel Dunstan, with his shrunken tissues and shrunken waistcoat regaining a martial ampleness, as the withered rose of Dr. Heidegger's experiment regained colour and perfume in the basin of Elixir of Youth, was wandering slowly about (for he never sat still) heaping food and conversation on Miss Flodden. He was informing her, among anecdotes of dead celebrities, reminiscences of Oriental warfare, principles of Persian colour arrangement, and panegyrics of virtuous incipient actresses, that Greenleaf was a capital fellow, although he would doubtless have been improved by military training; a scholar, and the son of a great scholar (Thomas Greenleaf's great edition of the "Mahabarata," which she should read some day when he, Colonel Dunstan, taught her Sanskrit), and that, for the rest, philanthropy, socialism, and the lower classes were a great mistake, of which the Ancient Persians would have made very short work indeed. To Greenleaf also he conveyed sundry information, not troubling to make it quite intelligible, for Colonel Dunstan considered that young men ought to be taught their place, which place was nowhere. So from various mutterings and ejaculations addressed to Miss Flodden, such as, "Ah, your great aunt, the duchess—what a woman she was! she had the shoulders of the Venus of Milo—I always told her she ought to ride out in the desert to excavate Palmyra with me;" and "that dear little cousin of yours—why didn't she let me teach her Arabic?" it became gradually apparent to Greenleaf that the old gentleman, who seemed as versed in Burke's Peerage and Baronetage as in cuneiform inscriptions, had known many generations of ladies of the house of Flodden. Nay, most unexpected of all, that the young lady introduced by Greenleaf had been a familiar object to the learned and hot-tempered Colonel ever since she had left the nursery. Greenleaf experienced a slight pang on this discovery: he had forgotten, in his own unworldliness, that worldly people like Colonel Dunstan and Miss Flodden probably moved in the same society.

"And your sister, how is she?" went on the old gentleman; "is she as bright as ever, now she is married, and has she got that little *air mutin* still? It's months since I've seen her; why didn't you bring her with you, my dear? And does *she* also take an interest in Rhodian pots, the dear, beautiful creature?"

Miss Flodden's face darkened as he slowly spun out his questions.

"I don't know what my sister is doing. I don't live with her any longer, Colonel Dunstan; and she is always busy rushing about with people; and I'm busy with pots and practising the fiddle; I've turned hermit since quite a long time."

"Well, well, practising the fiddle isn't a bad thing; Orpheus with his lute, you know. But you'd much better let me teach you Greek, my dear, and come to Asia Minor next winter with me. Lady Betty's coming, and we'll see what we can dig up among those sots of Turks. You can get capital tents at that fellow's—what's his name—in Piccadilly. And how are your people? I saw your brother Herbert the other day at a sale. He told me your father was determined not to let us have your collection, more's the pity! And what's become of that nice young fellow, Hermann Struwë, who used to be at your house? He hasn't got a wife yet, eh?"

Miss Flodden took no notice of these questions. She passed them over in disdainful silence, Greenleaf thought, till she suddenly said coldly:

"I should think Mr. Struwë will have no more difficulty in finding a wife than in hiring a shooting, or buying a sham antique."

She was a very beautiful woman, Greenleaf said to himself. She was very tall (Greenleaf wondered whether the women of that lot, of the idlers, were always a head taller than those of his acquaintance), and slender almost to thinness, with a rigid, undeveloped sort of grace which contrasted with the extreme composure—that sort of taking things for granted—of her manner. Old Mr. Dunstan had just alluded to her mother having been a Welshwoman; and Greenleaf thought he saw very plainly the Celt in this superficially Saxon-looking girl. That sharp perfection of feature—features almost over-much chiselled and finished in every minutest detail—that excessive mobility of mouth and eyes, did not belong to the usual kind of English pretty women. She was so much of a Celt, despite her Northumbrian name, that the pale-brown of her hair—hair crisp and close round her ears—gave him almost the impression of a wig; underneath it must really be jet black.

Notwithstanding a slight weariness at Colonel Dunstan's social reminiscences and questions, she seemed pleased and rather excited at finding herself in the sanctuary of his learning. While quietly taking care of the old gentleman, and much concerned lest he should stumble over chairs and footstools in his polite haverings, she let her eyes ramble over the expanse of books which covered the walls, evidently impressed by all that must be in them. And from the timid though pertinacious fashion in which she questioned him, it was clear that she thought him an oracle, although an oracle rather difficult to keep to the point.

"And now," she finally said, with a little suppressed desperation, "won't you show me some of the Rhodian ware, Colonel Dunstan? It would be so awfully good of you."

Colonel Dunstan suddenly unwrinkled himself with considerable importance. He had forgotten the Rhodian ware, and rather resented its existence. Why, bless you! *He* didn't possess such things as pots; and as to going to the Museum, it was the most cold-taking place in the world. He would show her his books some day, and the casts of the cuneiform inscriptions. She must come to tea again soon with him. Did she know Miss Tilly Tandem, who had just been engaged by Irving? He should like them to meet. That was her photograph.

"But," said Miss Flodden—Val Flodden it appeared she was called—"mayn't I—couldn't I—be allowed to see those Rhodian pots also?" She was dreadfully crestfallen, and had a little disappointed eagerness, like a child.

"Of course you can," Colonel Dunstan answered, with infinite disdain. "*I* don't think anything of Rhodian ware, you know—mere debased copy of the old Persian. Those Greeks of the islands were a poor lot, then as now. Believe me, those Greeks have always been a set of confounded liars and their account of Salamis will be set right some day. But if you want to see it, why of course you can. Greenleaf, take Miss Val Flodden to see the Rhodian ware some day soon; do you hear, Greenleaf, eh?"

"Yes, sir." Greenleaf had always said sir to Colonel Dunstan, like a little boy, or a subordinate. It made up for a kind of contempt with which the learned, but worldly and hot-tempered old gentleman very unreasonably inspired him. Greenleaf was full of prejudices, like all very gentle and apostolic persons.

"There's Greenleaf—go with him some morning," said Colonel Dunstan, regaining his temper; "but, bless me! Why haven't you had any more strawberries, Miss Val?"

III.

The discovery that he had introduced two people who had already been acquainted for years, depressed Greenleaf with something more than the mere sense of slight comicality. Indeed, Greenleaf, like many apostolic persons, was deficient in the sense of the comic, and destitute of all fear of social solecisms. As he waited under the portico of the Museum, the pigeons fluttering from the black temple frieze on to the sooty steps, and the rusty students pressing through the swinging glass doors, he felt a vague dissatisfaction—the sort of faint crossness common in children, and of which no contact with the world, the contact with its grating or planing powers, had cured this dreamer; but such crossness leaves in the candid mind a doubt of possible vicariousness, of being caused by something not its ostensible reason, or being caused by the quite undefinable. When at last, from out of the blue haze and gauzy blackness of the Bloomsbury summer, there emerged an object of interest, and the slender recognised figure detached itself from the crowd of unreal other creatures, on foot, in cabs, and behind barrows, he was aware of a certain flat and prosaic quality in things since that tea-party at Colonel Dunstan's. And he was very angry with himself, and consequently with everything else, when it struck him suddenly that perhaps he was annoyed at the little eccentric adventure—the adventure of the lady dropped from the clouds and never seen again—turning into a humdrum acquaintance, which might even linger on, with a girl about whose family he now knew everything, who, on her side, was now certain that he was a gentleman, and who did really and seriously intend to find out all about pots.

They walked quickly upstairs, exchanging very few words, save on the subject of umbrellas and umbrella tickets; and when they had arrived in the pottery room, they became wonderfully business-like. Miss Flodden was business-like simply because she was extraordinarily interested in the matter in hand; and Greenleaf was business-like because he was ashamed of having perhaps thought about Miss Flodden apart from pottery, and therefore most anxious, for his own moral dignity, to look at her and pottery as indissolubly connected.

As the narrator of this small history is unhappily an ignoramus on the subject of pottery, prudence forbids all attempt to repeat the questions of Miss

Flodden and the answers of Greenleaf on the subject of clay, colours, fixing glaze and similar mysteries. These were duly discussed for some time while the patient assistant unlocked case after case, and let them handle the great Hispano-Moorish dishes, heraldic creatures spreading wings among their arabesques of yellow brown goldiness; the rotund vases and ewers where Roman consuls and Jewish maidens and Greek gods were crowded together, yellow and green and brown, on the deep sea-blue of Castel Durante and Gubbio majolica; the fanciful scalloped blue upon blue nymphs and satyrs of seventeenth century Savona, which looked as if the very dishes and plates had wished to wear furbelows and perukes; and the precious pieces, cracked and broken, of Brusa tiles and Rhodian and Damascene platters, with the gorgeous crimson tulips—opening vistas of Oriental bean-fields—and fantastic green and blue fritillaries standing almost in relief on the thick white glaze.

"I suppose it's being brought up among the Yetholme collection that makes you know so much about pottery?" remarked Greenleaf, in considerable surprise: "you haven't been to this part of the Museum before?"

Miss Flodden raised her pale blue luminous eyes.

"Do you know, I've never been to the Museum since I was a tiny girl, at least, except once, when my married sister conducted a party of New York friends. I thought we were going to see stuffed birds, and I was so surprised to see all those beautiful Greek things—I had seen statues once when we went to Rome—I wanted so much to look at them a little, but my friends thought they weren't in good repair, and wanted to have tea and go to the park, so they scooted me round among the Egyptian things and the reading rooms and out by the door. Yes, the little I know I have learned by playing with our things at home. Some day you must see them, Mr. Greenleaf."

Greenleaf did not answer for a moment. Good heavens! here was a young woman of twenty-four or twenty-five who had spent part of every year of her life in London, and had been only once to the British Museum, and then had expected to see stuffed birds! And the girl apparently an instinctive artist, extraordinarily quick and just in her appreciations.

Then there were other things to do, besides opening galleries on Sundays and promenading East-end workmen in company with young men from Toynbee Hall! And Greenleaf's heart withered—as one's mouth withers at the contact of strong green tea or caper sauce—with indignation at all the waste of intellectual power and intellectual riches implied in this hideous present misarrangement of all things. Was it possible that the so-called upper classes, or at least some members thereof, were in one way as much the victims of injustice and barbarism as the lower classes, off whose labour they basely subsisted?

The thought came over him as his eyes met Miss Flodden's face—that delicately chiselled, mobile young face which was suddenly contracted with a smile of cynical, yet resigned bitterness. He made that reflection once more, when with the wand-bearing custodian imperturbably occupying the only seat in the place, they leaned upon the glass case, and she asked him, and he told her, about the various currents in art history—the form element of ancient Greece, the colour element of the Orientals, the patterns of Persian ware, the outline figures on Greek and Etruscan vases—things which he imagined every child to know, and about which, as about Greeks, Orientals, and Etruscans, and Latin and geography and most matters, this girl seemed completely ignorant.

"My word," she exclaimed, and that little piece of slang grated horribly on Greenleaf's nerves; "how very interesting things are when one knows something about them! Do you suppose all things would be equally interesting if one knew about them? Or would it only be every now and then, just as with other matters, balls, and picnics, and so forth? Or does one get interested whenever one does anything as hard as one can, like hard riding, or rowing, or playing tennis properly? Some books seem so awfully interesting, you know; but there are such a lot of others that one would just throw into the fire if they didn't belong to Mudie. But somehow a thread seems always to be wanting. It's like trying to play a game without knowing the rules. How have you got to know all these things, Mr. Greenleaf? I mean all the connections between things; and could anybody get the connecting links if they tried, or must one have a special vocation?"

Greenleaf was embarrassed how to answer. He really could not realise the extraordinary emptiness in this young woman's mind; and at the same time he felt strangely touched and indignant, as he did sometimes when giving some little street Arab a good thing which it had never eaten before, and did not clearly know how to begin eating.

"Have you—have you—never read at all methodically?" he asked. He really meant, "Have you never received any education?"

Miss Flodden reflected for a moment. "No. Somehow one never thought of reading as a methodical thing, as a business, you know. Dancing and hunting and playing tennis and seeing people, all that's a business, because one has to do it. At least one has to do it as long as one hadn't turned into a savage; everyone else has to do it. Of course, there's the fiddle; I've practised that rather methodically, but it was because I liked the sound of the thing so much, and I once had a little German—my brother's German crammer for diplomacy—who taught me. And then one knew that, unless one got up at five in the morning and did it regularly, it wouldn't be done at all. But reading is different. One just picks up a book before dinner, or while being dressed. And the books are usually such rot."

It was getting late, and Greenleaf conducted Miss Flodden back to her parasol, where it was waiting among the vast and shabby umbrellas of the studious, very incongruous in its semi-masculine, yet rather futile smartness, at the door of the reading-room.

"It is all very beautiful," remarked Miss Flodden, as they descended the Museum steps, with the pigeons fluttering all round in the dim, smoky air, nodding her head pensively.

"What?" asked Greenleaf. He had an almost conventual hatred of noise and bustle, which seemed to him, perhaps because he had elected to work among them, the utter profanation of life; and to his æsthetic soul, the fact that many thousands of people lived among smoke and smuts, and never saw a clear stream, a dainty meadow of grass and daisies, or a sky just washed into blueness by a shower, was one of the chief reasons for condemning modern industrial civilisation.

"Why, all that—the pale blue mist with the black houses quite soft, like black flakes against it, and the green of the trees against the black walls, and the moving crowd." Then, as if suddenly taking courage to say something rather dreadful, she said: "Tell me about Colonel Dunstan. Is he really so learned, does he know such a lot of things?"

Greenleaf laughed at the simplicity with which she asked this. She seemed to have a difficulty in realising that anyone could know anything.

"Yes, he knows a great lot of things. He is one of the first Orientalists in Europe, I believe—at least my father, who was an Oriental scholar himself, used to say so; and he is a great archæologist, besides his knowledge of Eastern things, and of course he knows more about Oriental art, and in fact all art, than almost anyone."

"Does he know," hesitated Miss Flodden, "what you were telling me about the different currents of ancient art, Persian and Greek and Etruscan, and the way in which artists lived then—all that you were telling me just now?"

Greenleaf laughed. "Good gracious, yes; I know nothing compared with him. Why, most of the little I know I learned at his lectures. Shall I hail that hansom for you, Miss Flodden?"

They were crossing Bedford Square. The birds were singing in the plane trees, and from the open windows of a solemn Georgian house, with its courses of white stone, and its classic door frieze, came the notes of a sonata of Mozart. All was wonderfully peaceful under the hazy summer sky.

"No—not yet. Tell me, then: since Colonel Dunstan knows so many interesting things, why in the world does he live like that?"

"Like what, Miss Flodden?"

"Why, as if—well, as if he knew nothing at all. Why does he go every afternoon a round of calls on silly women, gossiping about their dresses, and listening to all—well—the horrid, because it often *is* horrid, nonsense and filth people talk? I used to meet him about everywhere, when I used still to go into the world. He often came to my sister's—I thought he was just an old—well, an old creature like the rest of them, collecting gossip to retail it next door. Since he really knows all about beautiful things, why doesn't he stick to them—why does he go about with stupid folk—he must know lots of clever ones?"

"Because—because Colonel Dunstan is a man of the world," answered Greenleaf bitterly; "because he cares about art, and history, and philosophy, but he also cares for pretty women, and pretty frocks, and good manners, and white hands."

"But—why shouldn't one care—doesn't everyone care—for—well, good manners?"

He had spoken with such violence that Miss Flodden had turned round. Her question died away as she looked into his face. It had hitherto struck her merely by its great kindness, and a sort of gentle candour which was rare. Now, the clean-shaven features and longish hair gave her the impression of a fanatic priest, at least what she imagined such to be.

"In this world, as it now exists," continued Greenleaf in an undertone, which was almost a hiss, "things are so divided that a man must choose between people who are pretty and pleasant and well-mannered; and people who are ugly and brutish and hateful, because the first are idle and unjust, and the second overworked and oppressed. Nowadays, more even than when Christ taught it, a man cannot serve both God and Mammon; and God, at present, at least God's servants, live among the ignorant, and dirty, and suffering. Shan't I stop that hansom for you, Miss Flodden?"

"Yes," she answered with a catch in her breath, as if overcome by surprise, almost as by an attack.

"Good-bye," he said, closing the flaps of the hansom.

Miss Flodden's hand mechanically dropped on to one of them, and her head, with the little black bonnet all points and bows of lace, was looking straight into space, as one overcome by great astonishment.

Greenleaf sickened with shame at his vehemence.

"You will let me show you the Etruscan things some day?" he cried, as the hansom rolled off.

Ah, could he never, never learn to restrain himself? What business had he to talk of such things to such a woman. To let the holy of holies become, most likely, a subject of mere idle curiosity and idle talk?

IV.

As Greenleaf looked up from the article on the "Rochdale Pioneers and Co-operation" and glanced out of the window at the smoke-veiled, soot-engrained Northern towns, and the bleak-green North country hillsides which flashed past the express, he did not realise at all clearly that he was going to see once more Miss Val Flodden, and see her in the unexpected relations of hostess and guest.

She had indeed, during their last ramble through the British Museum, said something vague about his coming to Yetholme if ever he came North; but he had given the invitation no weight and had forgotten it completely. His journey was due to a circumstance more important in his eyes than the visit of a young lady to his studio, and would be crowned by an event far more satisfactory than the meeting with a stray acquaintance.

For Sir Percy Flodden had at last decided to sell the famous Yetholme collection of majolica and Palissy ware; and the South Kensington authorities had selected Leonard Greenleaf, potter and writer on pottery, to verify the catalogue and conclude the purchase. It was one of Greenleaf's socialist maxims that no important works of art should be hidden from public enjoyment in the houses of private collectors; an Act of Parliament, in his opinion, should force all owners to sell to the nation, supposing that arguments in favour of true citizenship and true love of art had failed to make them bestow their property gratis. Greenleaf had agitated during several years to induce the public to make the first bid for the Yetholme collection; difficulties of all kinds had stood in the way, and the owner himself had become restive in the negotiations; but now, at last, this immortal earthenware had been saved from further private collections and secured for the enjoyment of everybody.

This being the case, it was not wonderful if Miss Flodden was thrown into the shade by her family collection; and if Greenleaf had gradually got to think very little about her of late—I say of late, because until the Yetholme sale had diverted his mind from theory to practice, Miss Flodden had played a certain part in Greenleaf's thoughts. Her sudden intrusion upon the monotony of his existence had made him ponder once more upon his undergraduate's dream of reclaiming the upper as well as the lower classes; a dream which had gradually vanished before practical contact with the pressing want of the poor. He had forgotten, during the last five or six years, that the leisured classes existed otherwise than as oppressors of the overworked ones. But now there had returned to the surface his constitutional craving for harmony, his horror of class warfare, a horror all the greater that in this very gentle soul there was a possibility of intense hatred. Why should not the whole of society work out harmoniously a new and better social order? After all, he and his chosen friends belonged to the privileged class, and only the privileged class could give the generous initiative required to counteract the selfish claiming of rights from below. Mankind was not wicked and perverse; and the injustice, wantonness, and cruelty of the rich were, doubtless, a result of their ignorance: they must be shown that they could do without so many things and that other folk were wanting those things so very much. And, half consciously, the image of Val Flodden rose up to concentrate and typify the ideas she had evoked. She was the living example of the ignorance of all higher right and wrong, of all the larger facts of existence, in which the so-called upper classes lived on no better than heathen blacks.

In these reflections Greenleaf had never claimed for Miss Flodden any individual superiority: to do so would have been to diminish her value as a type and an illustration. She had become, in his thoughts, the natural woman as produced, or rather as destroyed, by the evil constitution of idle society. She appeared, indeed, to have a personal charm, but this was doubtless a class peculiarity which his inexperience perceived as an individual one. It was the sole business of idle folk, Greenleaf said to himself, to make themselves charming, and they doubtless carried this quality as high as blacksmiths do strength of arm, and sempstresses nimbleness of finger: for the occasional examples of idle folk without any charm at all quickly faded from Greenleaf's logical memory. Also, he forgot for the moment, that many women, neither ignorant nor idle, the three Miss Carpenters for instance, who lived in a servantless flat in Holborn and worked in the East End, had as much charm, though not quite the same; and that there were tricks of manner and speech, affectations of school-boy slang, yokel ways, about Miss Flodden herself, which affected his sensitive nerves as ungraceful. But, be this as it may, the acquaintance with Miss Flodden had set his thoughts on the disadvantages of the upper classes, and he found it convenient to use Miss Flodden as an illustration thereof.

Besides, every now and then, Greenleaf had felt, in those long talks at the Museum, a curious pang of pity for her. In Greenleaf's nature, more thoughtful than logical, the dominating forces were a kind of transcendent æstheticism, and an extraordinary, also transcendent, compassion—compassion which, coming upon him in veritable stabs, went to his head and soon passed the boundaries of individual pain and wrong. This man, who aspired towards the future and really hankered painfully after the past, was like some mediæval monk all quivering at the sufferings of a far-distant, impersonal Godhead, for the sake of whose wrongs he could even hate fiercely, and for the sake of whose more than individual sufferings he could feel, every now and then, overwhelming pity for some small, ill-treated bird, or beast, or man. That this girl—intelligent and good—had been brought up not merely in utter indifference to real evil (tempered only by a vague fear of a black man who carried you to hell and a much blacker man who turned you out of society) but in ignorance of every one of the nobler and more beautiful activities of life; this perception of moral and intellectual starvation, veiled his mind with tears and made him spiritually choke, like the sight of a supperless ragged child, or of a dog that had lost its master.

Such impressions had been common enough in their two or three meetings. They had met several times in the Museum, and once at Messrs. Boyce's works, the utter unworldliness of Greenleaf's mind preventing his asking himself, even once, whether such proceedings did not display unusual recklessness on the part of a girl belonging to Miss Flodden's set; so much that he did not even take heed of Miss Flodden's occasional remarks showing that this liberty, this familiarity with a man and a stranger, were possible only because she had deliberately turned her back on her former companions. Indifferent to personal matters, he had not even understood very plainly (although he had a pleasant, vague sense of something similar) that unfamiliarity with the class and type to which he belonged had given the girl a sense of absolute safety which allowed her to go about and discuss everything with this man from a different sphere, as she might have done with another woman. This knowledge was vague and scarce conscious, taking the form rather of indignation with Miss Flodden's world and pity for Miss Flodden's self, whenever, incidentally, she said things which revealed the habit of an opposite state of things, the habit of a woman's liberty of action, speech and feeling being cramped by disbelief in men's purity and honour, or rather by knowledge of their thinly varnished baseness.

Thus it had come about during that dim and delicate London June that the young lady from Eaton Square had become a familiar figure in the mind, if not in the life, of the Socialist potter of Church Street, Bloomsbury. There was, of course, a certain exotic strain in the matter; and as they rambled among the solemn sitting Pharaohs, the Roman Emperors and headless Greek demigods, and the rows of glass cases in the cool, empty Museum, Greenleaf occasionally experienced, while discussing various forms of art and describing dead civilisations, a little shock of surprise on realising the nature of his companion, on catching every now and then an intonation and an expression which told of ball-rooms and shooting-houses, on perceiving suddenly, silhouetted against the red wall, or reflected in a glass case, the slender, dapper figure in its plain, tight clothes; the tight, straight-featured head beneath its close little bonnet. But this sense of the unusual and the exotic was subdued by the sense of the real, the actually present, just as, in some foreign or Eastern town, our disbelief in the possibility of it all is oddly moulded into a sort of familiarity by the knowledge that we are our ourselves, and ourselves are on the spot.

It was different now; as his train jogged slowly along the banks of the Tweed, between the bare, green hills and the leafy little ravines of Northumberland. A couple of months' separation had gradually reduced Miss Flodden to an unfamiliar, and almost an abstract being. She was the subject no longer of impressions, but merely of reflections; and of reflections which had grown daily more general, as the perfume of individuality faded away. Greenleaf lived so much more in his thoughts than in his life that creatures very speedily got to represent nothing but problems to him. At this moment his main interest in life was to secure the Yetholme collection of majolica and Palissy work; the fact that he was going, in a few minutes, to meet Miss Flodden was not more important than the fact that he would have to get his portmanteau out of the van. And as to Miss Flodden, she represented to him, in a rather rubbed-out way, the problem of upper class want of education and moral earnestness.

It seemed to him also, as he shook hands with Miss Flodden, in her cart at Yetholme station, and took his place beside her in the vehicle, that not only all his own feelings about Miss Flodden, but Miss Flodden herself had changed. She had grown so much more like everybody else, he thought, or he had got to see her so much more in her reality. There was nothing exotic about her now, wrapped in a big, fuzzy cloak, a big cap drawn over her head, concealing the close, light-brown curls, and making her face so very much less keen in feature. He wondered why he had seen so much of the Celt in her, and such a far-fetched nervous fineness. She seemed also, in her almost monosyllabic conversation, mainly preoccupied with his portmanteau, the hours of his train, the names of the villages and hills they passed, and similar commonplace matters; whereas, in London he had noted the eager insistence with which she had immediately set the conversation and firmly kept it on intellectual and artistic problems.

The cart rolled away by high-lying fields of pale green barley and oats shivering in the cold breeze, between the stunted hedges, whence an occasional wind-warped thorn-tree rose black against the pale yellow afternoon sky, with every now and then a bunch of blue cranesbill, or a little fluttering group of poppies, taking the importance of bushes and trees in this

- 65 -

high, bleak, Northern country. Great savage dogs, with chests and pointed ears like the antique Cerberus, came barking out of the black stone cottages; and over the fields, from the tree-tops just visible in the river valley below, circled innumerable rooks, loudly cawing. The road made a sudden dip, and they were on a level with the wide, shingly bed of the Tweed, scattered sheep grazing along the banks. Then a black belfry appeared among black ash trees; a row of black cottages bordered the road with their hollyhocks and asters; and the cart rolled in between rows of rook-peopled trees, and stopped at last before a long, black stone house, sunk, as in some parts of Scotland, into a kind of trench. There was a frightful alarum of dogs of all kinds, rushing up from all directions. But Miss Flodden led Greenleaf into the house and through various passages, without any human being appearing, save a boy, to whom she threw the reins at the door. At last, in a big, dark drawing-room, a child was discovered helping herself to milk and bread and jam at a solitary table.

"They're all out," she said, taking no notice of Greenleaf, although scanning him with the critical eyes of six or seven. "Cut me a scone, Val, and put butter on it, but not too much."

"This is a step-sister of mine," explained Miss Flodden, laconically, nodding in the child's direction, as she threw aside her cloak, drew off her gloves, and began pouring out tea. "I say, leave that scone alone until I can cut it for you. It's rather hard lines on one for the family to have its tea and leave us only the cold dregs."

She looked listless and calm and bored. Greenleaf wondered how he could ever have romanced about this handsome, commonplace young woman. Then he began to speculate as to where the famous collection was kept.

V.

"It's very unfair of me, of course," Miss Flodden remarked next morning, as she handed down plate after plate, jar after jar, to Greenleaf, seated, the catalogue before him and the pen in his hand, at a long deal table—"it's very unfair, and it isn't at all business, but I used to think I should like to see you again; and now, on account of these pots, I dislike you."

Greenleaf looked up in astonishment. It was as if the veil of sullenness, preventing his recognition of Miss Flodden ever since his arrival, had suddenly been torn asunder by a burst of passion. The girl was standing by the glass case, dusting a Limoges platter with a feather brush, her mannish coat and short skirt covered with dust. She spoke in an undertone, and her eyes were looking down upon the platter; but it struck him at once that she was a Celt once more, and that the Celtic waywardness and emotion were bursting out the more irresistibly for that long repression due to the Spartan undemonstrativeness of smart society. He noticed also a trait he had forgotten, and which had seemed to be, long ago at the Museum, a sort of mark of temperament, telling of inherited ferocity in this well-bred young lady; two of her little white teeth, instead of being square pearls, like their companions, were pointed and sharp, like those of a wild animal. And as she raised her eyes, their light, whitish blue, flashed angrily.

"Excuse my being so rude, Mr. Greenleaf," she added very coldly, "you have been so good, showing and explaining a lot of things to me, that it's only fair you should know that, on account of the pots, I have—well, got to dislike you. You see," she went on, turning her back to him, "they were my toys. They were the only people, except the trees and the river, one had to talk to sometimes."

Greenleaf had noticed at dinner last night, and again this morning at lunch, that Miss Flodden seemed to have very little in common with her family, and, indeed, scarcely any communication at all.

Sir Percy Flodden, an old gentleman with a beautiful white beard, and beautiful soft manners, but a deficiency in further characteristics, had found leisure, in the intervals of organising Primrose meetings, making speeches at Conservative dinners, writing letters to the *Times* about breeds of cattle, and hunting and fishing a great deal, to get married a second time, and to produce a large number of younger fishermen and huntresses, future Primrose Leaguers and writers to the *Times*. The second wife being dead, and sundry aunts installed in her place, the younger generation of Floddens, after gradually emerging from the nursery, ran wild in brooks and streams, stables and haylofts, until the boys were packed off to civilisation and Eton, pending further civilisation and Sandhurst; and the girls were initiated into their proper form of civilisation by being taken to a drawing-room and then hustled into further female evolution by an energetic and tactful married sister. The elder girls were now at home, preparing clothes for various balls and packing trunks for various visits; and the elder boys had come back on holidays, with fishing-rods, coin collections, the first three books of Euclid, and the last new thing in slang; as to the younger half-brothers and sisters, they were still in the phase of the hayloft and stable, emerging only to partake of gigantic breakfasts and teas.

Among all these good-natured and well-mannered, but somewhat dull creatures, Val Flodden moved in an atmosphere of her own, somewhat of a stranger, considerably of a puzzle, and regarded with the mixed awe and suspicion due to her having been recently an admittedly pretty woman, and now showing signs of becoming an undoubtedly eccentric one. Besides, there was the fact that Val Flodden was partially a Celt, and that her father and brothers were most emphatically Saxons.

All this it has been necessary to explain that the reader might understand that Greenleaf might have understood Miss Flodden's passionate clinging to her sole companions at Yetholme, the old crockery of her grandfather's collection.

But although Greenleaf did actually take in a portion of the situation, he was mainly impressed by the want of public spirit exhibited by the young lady; so inevitably do we expect other folk to possess even our most eccentric standards, and to rule their feelings and actions by notions of which they have probably never even heard.

Miss Flodden had broken through all rules in manifesting her feelings about the pots; Greenleaf never dreamed of taking advantage of her false move, but with his usual simplicity, encouraged by a plain-spokenness, which never struck him as otherwise than natural, he answered very gravely: "Of course I understand how fond you must be of these beautiful things, and how much it must have been to you—it would be to anyone who cared for art, even if not specially interested like you in pottery—to have them constantly before you. But you ought to remember that you are parting with them for the advantage of others."

Miss Flodden flushed a little. It was probably from surprise and shame at this man's stupidity. She must have felt as if she herself had alluded to the necessity of selling these heirlooms, as if she herself had done the incredible thing of pointing out the pecuniary advantage. Then, apparently, she reflected that if this man was so obtuse, he could not help himself; but that he was doubtless honest in his intentions. For she added coldly, and hiding her contemptuous face from him with a jar held at arms' length:

"Of course I know that it's for the benefit of my brothers and sisters. I don't grudge them the money, heaven knows, and when one's broke, one's broke. Only it's sad to think what sort of things—what stupid amusements and useless necessaries these lovely things will be exchanged for, merely because the world is so idiotically constituted. You see, the possession of these pots ought to give everyone more pleasure than the possession of an additional horse, or an extra frock."

Greenleaf was as much taken aback at her misconception of his meaning as she had been at her supposed understanding of it.

"Good gracious, Miss Flodden, I didn't mean the advantage of your brothers and sisters. But surely you ought to reflect that these pots passing from a private house in Northumberland to the South Kensington Museum, will mean that hundreds of people will be afforded pleasure, instead of only one or two—one, namely yourself, by your own account. Besides, do you really think that any private individual has a moral right to keep for himself any object capable of giving a noble kind of pleasure to his fellows, merely because the present state of society allows him to possess more money than his neighbours, and to lock up things as his property? Surely art belongs to all who can enjoy it!"

There was something fault-finding in Greenleaf's tone, owing to the fact that he could not realise such ideas, so very familiar to himself, not being equally familiar to everyone else.

Miss Flodden set down the jar she was dusting, keeping her wrist balanced on its edge, and looked at Greenleaf with surprise in her blue eyes, which concentrated, and seemed to grow darker and deeper by the concentration.

"Really," she asked incredulously, "are you speaking seriously? But then— what would become of luxury and so forth?"

"The active would enjoy it as well as the idle—or rather, there would be no longer either active or idle; everyone would work and enjoy equally, and equally fairly and rationally."

"Then," went on Miss Flodden slowly, the sequence of thoughts bursting with difficulty on to her mind, "no one would have things, except for real enjoyment and as a result of fairly earning them? People would all have books and beautiful trees and fields to look at, and pictures and music; but no diamonds, or stepping horses, or frocks from Worth—the things one has because other folk have them."

Greenleaf smiled: she seemed to him, talking of these things which "one" had because "others" had them, things so futile, so foreign to his mind, extraordinarily like a child talking of the snakes, whales, and ogres, represented by tables and chairs, and hearthrugs.

"Of course not."

"At that rate," went on the girl, "there would no longer be any need for marrying and giving in marriage. One would live quite free; free to work at what one liked, and look about without folks worrying one."

Greenleaf did not follow her thought, for his own thoughts were too foreign to the habits she was alluding to.

"I don't see," he added simply, "why people shouldn't marry or be given in marriage because every one worked and had leisure. Some mightn't, perhaps, because some would always, perhaps, want to work too much, and because things matter to me—I mean to some—more than other people. But I can't see why others shouldn't marry and be given in marriage, Miss Flodden."

A little contraction passed across the girl's face, and she answered in a hurried, husky voice:

"No, no; that would be all over."

And they fell again to the catalogue. It was a very hard day's work, that first one, for the catalogue was in horrid confusion; and they really could not have had time to talk much about other things, for they went on with merely a brief space for lunch, and Greenleaf was sent for a walk with one of the boys at tea time, while Miss Flodden unwillingly entertained some neighbours. Then at dinner the conversation, in which she took no part, rolled mainly upon local pedigrees, crops, how many fish the boys had caught, in what houses friends were staying, whom sundry young ladies of the neighbourhood were likely to marry, and how many bags had been made at the various shoots. Still, despite these irrelevant interests, Miss Flodden seemed to have understood why Greenleaf had expected her to like the sale of the collection, and Greenleaf to have understood why Miss Flodden should have been vexed at the collection being sold. At least there was a sense of mutual comprehension and good-will, such as the morning had scarcely promised. And when, after fretting a little over more bags of game and more local pedigrees, with his host and the boys after dinner, Greenleaf returned to find the ladies in various stages of somnolence, over the drawing-room fire; he experienced an odd sense of the naturalness of things when Miss Flodden asked whether he could play the piano, and took her violin out of its case.

Miss Flodden did not play exactly well, for it appears that very few people do; and she, of course, had had but little opportunity of learning. Yet, in a way, she played the fiddle much better, Greenleaf felt, than he himself, who was decidedly a proficient, could play the piano. For there was in her playing the expression not merely of talent, but of extraordinary, passionate, dogged determination to master the instrument. It was as much this as the actual execution which gave the charm to her performance. To Greenleaf the charm was immense. He nearly always played, when he did play, with men; and he hated the way in which the fiddle crushes the starched hideous shirt, the movement of bowing rucks the black sleeve and hard white cuff too high above the red, masculine wrist; and among the dreams of his life there had always been a very silly one, of a younger sister—he always thought of her as called Emily—who would have learned the violin, and who would have stood before him like this, bow in hand, while he looked up from his piano. It seems odd, perhaps, that the fair violinist should never have appeared to his mind as a possible wife; but so it was. And so it was that this image, which had dawned upon his school-boy fancy long before the delectableness of marriage could ever be understood, and when his solitary little soul still smarted at his dull, grown-up, companionless home—so it was that the image of "Emily"—the imaginary sister with the violin—had gradually taken the place in his heart of that grave Miss Delia Carpenter, the only woman whom he had ever loved, and who had told him she was in love with another.

The family was beginning to disperse; the girls to wake up yawning from their novels or their embroidery; the father to start suddenly from his slumber over the *Times*; the boys, having satisfied themselves in the newspapers about the number of brace of grouse, had sneaked off to prepare flies for the next day's fishing; and still the duet went on, the image of "Emily" gradually acquiring the blue eyes (its own had been brownish) and clear-cut, nervous features (she had hitherto had an irregular style of beauty) of Val Flodden.

"That's enough," said Miss Flodden, putting her violin tenderly—she had the same rather unwonted tenderness with some of the majolica—into its case, and looking round at the sleepy faces of the family. "Jack, give Mr. Greenleaf his candle. And," she added, as they shook hands, "you'll tell me some more about how it will be when everybody works and has leisure, won't you, to-morrow?"

That night Greenleaf saw in his dreams his father's rectory among the south country pines, the garden and paddock, the big library and loft full of books; and among it all there wandered about, rather dim in features, but unhesitatingly recognised, that imaginary sister, the violinist Emily.

VI.

"Tell me more about the Miss Carpenters," said Miss Flodden shyly, keeping her eyes fixed on the rapidly flowing twist of water between the big shingle, where every now and then came the spurt of a salmon's leap.

They were seated, after tea, and another hard day's cataloguing, under some beech trees that overhung the Tweed. From the fields opposite—no longer England, already Scotland—came the pant and whirr of a threshing-machine; while from the woods issued the caw of innumerable rooks, blackening the sky. A heron rose from among the reeds of the bank, and mounted, printing the pale sky with his Japanese outline. There was incredible peacefulness, not unmixed with austerity, in the gurgle of the water, the green of the banks, the scent of damp earth.

Greenleaf, who was very reserved about his friends, so much that one friend might almost have imagined him to possess no others, had somehow slid into speaking of his little Bloomsbury world to this girl, who was so foreign to it. It had come home to him how utterly Miss Flodden had lived out of contact with all the various concerns of life, and out of sight of the people who have such. Except pottery and violin music, come into her existence by the merest accident, and remaining there utterly isolated, she had no experience, save of the vanities of the world. But what struck him most, and seemed to him even more piteous, was her habit of regarding these vanities as matters not of amusement, but of important business. To her, personally, it would seem, indeed, that frocks, horses, diamonds, invitations to this house or that, and all the complications of social standing, afforded little or no satisfaction. But then she accepted the fact of being an eccentric, a creature not quite all it should be; and she expected everyone else to be different, to be seriously engaged in the pursuit of the things she, personally, and owing to her eccentricity, did not want.

It was extraordinary how, while she expressed her own distaste for various weaknesses and shortcomings, she defended those who gave way to them as perfectly normal creatures. Greenleaf was horrified to hear her explain, with marvellous perception of how and wherefore, and without any blame, the manner in which women may gradually allow men not their husbands to pay their dressmaker's bills, and gradually to become masters of their purse and of themselves: the necessity of a new frock at some race or ball, the desire to outshine another woman, to get into royalty's notice, and the fear of incensing a husband already hard up—all this seemed to Miss Flodden perfectly natural and incontrovertible; and she pleaded for those who gave way under such pressure.

"Of course I wouldn't do it," she said, twisting a long straw in her hands; "it strikes me as bad form, don't you know; but then I'm peculiar, and there are so many things in the world which other folk don't mind, and which I can't bear. I don't like some of their talk, and I don't like their not running quite straight. But then I seem to have been born with a skin less than one ought to have."

Greenleaf listened in silent horror. In the course of discussing how much the world might be improved by some of his socialistic plans, this young lady of four or five and twenty had very simply and quietly unveiled a state of corruption, of which, in his tirades against wealth and luxury, he had had but the vaguest idea. "You see," Miss Flodden had remarked, "it's because one has to have so many things which one's neighbours have, whether they give one much pleasure or not, that a woman gets into such false positions, which make people, if things get too obvious, treat her in a beastly, unjust way. But women have always been told that they *must* have this and that, and go to such and such a house, otherwise they'd not keep up in it all; and then they're fallen upon afterwards. It's awfully unfair. Why, of course, if one hadn't always been told that one *must* have frocks, and carriages, and *must* go to Marlborough House, one wouldn't get married. Of course it's different with me, because I'm queer, and I like making pots, and am willing to know no one. But then that's all wrong, at least my married sister is always saying so. And, of course, I'm not going to marry, however much they bore me about it."

"You speak as if women got married merely for the sake of living like their neighbours," remarked Greenleaf; "that's absurd."

Miss Flodden, seated on a stone, looked up at him under his beech tree. Her face bore a curious expression of incredulity dashed with contempt. Could he be a Pharisee?

"There may be exceptions," she answered, "and perhaps you may know some. But if a woman were secure of her living, and did not want things, why should she get married?" It was as if she had said, Why should a Hindoo widow burn herself? "There must be some inducement," she added, looking into the water and plucking at the grass, "to give oneself into the keeping of another person." Her face had that same contraction, as once when she had mentioned the matter before.

"Good God," thought Greenleaf, "into what ugly bits of life had this girl been forced to look!" And he felt a great pity and indignation about things in general.

Miss Flodden sent a stone skimming across the river, as if to dismiss the subject, and then it was that she said rather hesitatingly:

"Tell me more about the Miss Carpenters."

She had an odd, timid curiosity about Greenleaf's friends, about everyone who did anything, as if she feared to intrude on them even in thought.

Greenleaf had spoken about them before and not unintentionally. These three sisters, living in their flat off Holborn, doing all their housework themselves, and yet finding time to work among the poor, to be cultivated and charming, were a stalking horse of his, an example he liked to bring before this member of fast society.

He had taken his refusal by one of the sisters with a philosophy which had astonished himself, for he certainly had thought that Delia was very dear to him. She was dear in a way now. But he felt quite pleased at her marriage with young Farquhar of the Museum, and he rather enjoyed talking about her. He told Miss Flodden of Maggie Carpenter's work among the sweaters, and of the readings of English literature she and Clara gave to the shop-girls;

and he was a little shocked, when he told her of the young woman from Shoolbred's who had borrowed a volume of Webster, that Val Flodden had never heard of that eminent dramatist, and thought he was the dictionary. He described the little suppers they gave in their big kitchen, where the one or two guests helped to lay the table and to wash up afterwards, previous to going to the highest seats in the Albert Hall, or to some socialist lecture; then the return on foot through the silent, black Bloomsbury streets. He made it sound even more idyllic than it really was. Then he spoke of Delia and the piano lessons she gave and the poems she wrote. He even repeated two of the poems out loud and felt that they were very beautiful.

"They can never bore themselves," remarked Miss Flodden, pensively.

"Bore themselves?" responded Greenleaf.

"Yes: bore themselves and feel they just *must* have something different to think about, like birds beating against cage bars." Then, after a pause, she said vaguely and hesitatingly: "I wish there were a chance for one to know the Miss Carpenters."

Greenleaf brightened up. This was what he wished. "Of course you shall know them, if you care, Miss Flodden, only——;"

"Only—you mean that they would think me a bore and an intruder."

"No," answered Greenleaf, he scarcely knew why, "that's not what I meant. But you must remember that you and they belong to different classes of society."

Miss Flodden's face contracted. "Ah," she exclaimed angrily. "Why must you throw that in my face? You have said that sort of thing several times before. Why do you?"

Why, indeed? For Greenleaf could not desist, every now and then, from bringing up that fact. It made the girl quiver, but he could not help himself; it was an attempt to find out whether she was really in earnest, which he occasionally doubted; and also it was a natural reaction against certain cynical assumptions, certain takings for granted on Miss Flodden's part that the vanity and corruption of her miserable little clique permeated the whole of the world—of the world which did not even know, in many instances, that there was such a thing as a smart lot!

But now he was sorry.

"Indeed," he said sorrowfully, "such a gulf between classes unfortunately still exists. In our civilisation, where luxury and the money which buys it go for so much, those who work must necessarily be separate from those who play."

"Heaven knows you have no right to abuse us for having money," exclaimed Miss Flodden, much hurt. "Why, if I don't get married, and I shan't, I shall never have a penny to bless myself with."

"It's a question of the lot one belongs to," answered Greenleaf unkindly; but added, rather remorsefully: "Would you like me to give you a letter for the Miss Carpenters when next you go to town? I have," he hesitated a little, "talked a good deal about you with them."

"Really!" exclaimed Miss Flodden quickly. "That's awfully good of you—I mean to give me a letter—only I fear it will bore them. I shall be going to town for a week or two in October. May I call on them then, do you think?"

"Of course." And Greenleaf, who was a business-like man, drew out his pocket-book, full of little patterns for pots and notes for lectures, and wrote on a clean page:

"Mem.: Letter for the Miss Carpenters for Miss Flodden."

"I will write it to-night or to-morrow; you shall have it before I leave. By the way, that train the day after to-morrow is at 6.20, is it not?"

"Yes," answered Miss Flodden. "I wish you could stay longer."

And they walked home.

As they wandered through the high-lying fields of green oats and yellow barley, among whose long beards the low sun made golden dust, with the dark, greenish Cheviots on one side, purple clouds hanging on their moor sides, and the three cones of the Eildons rising, hills of fairy-land, faint upon the golden sunset mist—as they wandered talking of various things, pottery, philosophy, and socialism, Greenleaf felt stealing across his soul a peacefulness as unlike his usual mood, as this northern afternoon, with soughing grain and twittering of larks, was different from the grime and bustle of London. He knew, now, that Miss Delia Carpenter's refusal had been best for him; his nature was too thin to allow of his giving himself both to a wife and family, and to the duties and studies which claimed him; he would have starved the affections of the first while neglecting the second. His life must always be a solitary one with his work. But into this rather cheerless solitude, there seemed to be coming something, he could scarcely tell what. Greenleaf believed in the possible friendship between a man and a woman; if it had not existed often hitherto, that was the fault of our corrupt bringing up. But it was possible and necessary; a thing different from, more perfect and more useful, than any friendship between persons of the same sex. But more different still, breezier, more robust and serene, than love even at its best. And had he not always wished for that sister, that Emily who had never existed? Of course he did not contemplate seeing very much of Miss

Flodden; still less did he admit to himself that this strange, reserved, yet outspoken girl might be the friend he craved for. But he felt a curious satisfaction, despite his better reason, which protested against everything abnormal, and which explained a great deal by premature experience of the world's ugliness—he felt a satisfaction at Miss Flodden's aversion to marriage. He could not have explained why, but he knew in a positive manner that this girl never had been, and never would be, in love; that this young woman of a frivolous and fast lot, was a sort of female Hippolytus, but without a male Diana; and he held tight to the knowledge as to a treasure.

VII.

The next day, Greenleaf was a little out of conceit with himself and the world at large: a vague depression and irritation got hold of him. Before breakfast, while ruminating over a list of books for Miss Flodden's reading, he had mechanically taken up a volume which lay on the drawing-room table. There were not many books at Yetholme, except those which were never moved from the library shelves; and the family's taste ran to Rider Haggard and sporting novels; while the collection put in his room, and bearing the name of *Valentine Flodden*, consisted either of things he already knew by heart—a selection from Browning, a volume of Tolstoy, and an Imitation of Christ;— or of others—as sundry works on Esoteric Buddhism, a handbook of Perspective, and a novel by Marie Corelli—which he felt little desire to read. The book that he took up was from the Circulating Library, Henry James's "Princess Casamassima." He had read it, of course, and dived into it—the last volume it was—at random. Do authors ever reflect how much influence they must occasionally have, coming by accident, to arouse some latent feeling, or to reinforce some dominant habit of mind? Certainly Henry James had been possessed of no ill-will towards Miss Val Flodden, whom indeed he might have made the heroine of some amiable story. Yet Henry James, at that moment, did Val Flodden a very bad turn. Greenleaf got up from the book, after twenty minutes' random reading, in a curiously suspicious and aggressive mood. Of course he never dreamed that he, a gentleman of some independent means, a scholar, a man who had known the upper classes long before he had ever come in contact with the lower, could have anything in common with poor Hyacinth, the socialist bookbinder, pining for luxury and the love of a great lady; neither was there much resemblance between Christina Light, married to Prince Casamassima, and this young Val Flodden married to nobody; yet the book depressed him horribly, by its suggestion of the odd freaks of curiosity which relieve the weariness of idle lives. And the depression was such, that he could not hold his tongue on the subject.

"Have you read that book—the 'Princess Casamassima'—Miss Flodden?" he asked at breakfast.

"Yes," answered the girl; "isn't it good? and so natural, don't you think?"

"You don't mean that you think the Princess natural—you don't think there ever could be such a horrible woman?"

He was quite sure there might be, indeed the fear of such an one quite overpowered him at this very moment; and he asked in hopes of Miss Flodden saying that there were no Princess Casamassimas.

Something in his tone appeared to irritate Miss Flodden. She thought him pharisaical, as she sometimes did, and considered it her duty to give him a setting down with the weight of her superior worldly wisdom.

"Of course I think her natural; only she might be more natural still."

"You mean more wicked?" asked Greenleaf sharply.

"No, not more wicked. The woman in the book may be intended to be wicked; but she needn't have been so in real life. Not at all wicked. She's merely a clever woman who is bored by society, and who wants to know about a lot of things and people. Heaps of women want to know about things because they're bored, but it's not always about nice things and nice people, as in the case of the Princess. She may have done mischief—she shouldn't have played with that wretched little morbid bookbinding boy; women oughtn't to play with men even when they're fools, indeed especially not then. But that wasn't inevitable. Hyacinth *would* run under her wheels. Of course I shouldn't have cared for that chemist creature either, nor for that Captain Sholto; he behaved rather like a cad all round, don't you think? But after all, they all talked very well; about interesting things—real, important things—didn't they?"

"And you think that to hear people talk about *real, important things* is a great delight, Miss Flodden?" asked Greenleaf, with a bitterness she did not fully appreciate.

"You would understand it if you had lived for years among people who talked nothing but gossip and rot," she answered sadly, rising from her place.

No more was said that morning about the Princess Casamassima. Miss Flodden was rather silent during their cataloguing work, and Greenleaf felt vaguely sore, he knew not what about.

Throughout the day, there kept returning to his mind those words, "You see they talked very well, about interesting things, important, *real* things, didn't they?" and the simple, taking-things-for-granted tone in which they had been said. Women of her lot, Miss Flodden had once informed him, would go great lengths for the sake of a new frock or a pair of stepping horses. Was it not possible that some of them, to whom frocks and horses had been offered in too great abundance, might transfer their desire for novelty to interesting talk and *real* things?

That was their last afternoon together. The catalogue had been finished with. Miss Flodden took Greenleaf for a drive in her cart. They sped along under the rolling clouds of the blustering northern afternoon, the rooks, in black swarms, cawing loudly, and the pee-wits screeching among the stunted hedges and black stones of the green, close-nibbled pastures; it was one of those August days which foretell winter. Greenleaf could never recollect very well what they had talked about, except that it had been about a great variety of things, which the blustering wind had seemed to sweep away like the brown beech leaves in the hollows. The fact was that Greenleaf was not attending. He kept revolving in his mind the same idea, with the impossibility of solving it. He was rather like a man in love, who cannot decide whether or not he is sufficiently so to make a declaration and feels the propitious moment escaping. Greenleaf was not in love; had he been, had there been any chance of his being so, Val Flodden would not have been there in the cart by his side; she had once told him, in one of her fits of abstract communicativeness, that people in love were despicable, but for that reason to be pitied, and that to let them fall in love was to be unkind to them, and to prepare a detestable exhibition for oneself. So Greenleaf was not in love. But he was as excited as if he had been. He felt that a great suspicion had arisen within him; and that this suspicion was about to deprive him of a friendship to which he clung as to a newly-found interest in life.

About Miss Flodden he did not think—that is to say, whether he might be running the risk of depriving *her* of something. He had not made love to her, so what could he deprive her of? Besides he thought of Miss Flodden exclusively as of the person who was probably going to deprive him of something he wanted. Deprive him if his suspicions should be true. For if his suspicions were true, there was no alternative to giving up all relations with her. He was not a selfish man, trying to save himself heartburns and disenchantments. He was thinking of his opinions, solely. It was quite impossible that they should become the toys of an idle, frivolous woman. Such a thing could not be. The sense of sacrilege was so great that he did not even say to himself that such a thing could *not be allowed*: to him it took the form of impossibility of its being at all.

Greenleaf was in an agony of doubt; he kept on repeating to himself—"Is she a Princess Casamassima?" so often, that at last he found it quite natural to put the question, so often formulated internally, out loud to her. Of course if she were a Princess Casamassima, her denial would be worth nothing; but when we cannot endure a suspicion against someone, we do not, in our wild desire to have it denied at any price, stop short to reflect that the denial will be worthless. A denial; he wanted a denial, not for the sake of justice towards her, but for his own peace of mind. He was on the very point of putting that strange question to her, when, in the process of a conversation in which he had taken part as in a dream, there suddenly came the unasked-for answer.

They must have been talking of the Princess Casamassima again, and of the uninterestingness of most people's lives. Greenleaf could not remember. It was all muddled in his memory, only there suddenly flashed a sentence, distinct, burning, out of that forgotten confusion.

"It's odd," said Miss Flodden's high, occasionally childish voice; "but I've always found that the people who bored one least were either very clever or very fast."

They were clattering into a little border town, with low black houses on either side, and a square tower, with a red tile extinguisher, and a veering weather-cock, closing the distance and connecting the grey, wet flags below with the grey, billowy sky above.

Greenleaf, although forgetful of all save theories, remembered for a long time that street and that tower. He did not answer, for his heart was overflowing with bitterness.

So it was true; and it just had to be. He had let his belief become the plaything of a capricious child. He had lost his dear friend. It was inevitable.

Greenleaf did not say a word, and showed nothing until his departure. But his letter to Miss Flodden, thanking for the hospitality of Yetholme, was brief, and it contained no allusion to any future meeting, and no promised introduction to the Miss Carpenters. Only at the end was this sentence: "I have lately been re-reading Henry James's 'Princess Casamassima': and I agree with you completely now as to the naturalness of her character."

VIII.

Some ten years later found Leonard Greenleaf once more—but this time with only a brougham and a footman to meet him—on his way to stay in a country house. He had been left penniless by his attempts to start co-operative workshops: and overwork and worry had made him far too weak to be a tolerable artisan; so, after having given up his pottery, those long years ago, because it ministered exclusively to rich men's luxury, he had been obliged to swallow the bitterness of perfecting rich men's dwellings in the capacity of Messrs. Boyce & Co.'s chief decorator; and now he was bent upon one of these hated errands.

Time, and the experience of many failures, had indeed perplexed poor Greenleaf's socialistic schemes a little, and had left him doubtful how to hasten the millennium, except by the slow methods of preaching morality and thrift; but time had rather exasperated his hatred of the idleness and selfishness of the privileged classes, to whose luxury he now found himself a minister. And, as he looked out of his window while dressing for dinner (those evening clothes, necessary for such occasions, had become a badge of servitude in his eyes), he felt that old indignation arise with unaccountable strength, and choke him with his own silence. It was a long, low house, the lawn spread, with scarcely any fall, down to the river brink; a wide band of green, then a wide band of shimmering, undecided blue and grey, reflecting the coppery clouds and purple banks of loose-strife, and then beyond and higher up in the picture, flat meadows, whose surface was beginning to be veiled in mist, and whose boundary elms were growing flat and unsubstantial, like painted things. There were birds twittering, and leaves rustling: a great sense of peacefulness, for the family and guests were doubtless within doors busy dressing. Suddenly, there was a plash of oars, and a peal of laughter; and, after a minute, two men and a woman came hurrying up the green lawn, against whose darkening slopes their white clothes made spots of unearthly whiteness in the twilight. They were noisy, and Greenleaf hated their laughter; but suddenly the lady stopped short a moment, and said to her companions in a tone of boredom and irritation: "Oh, shut up; can't you let one look about and listen to things once in a way?"

There was more laughter, and they all disappeared indoors. Greenleaf leaned upon his window, wondering where he had heard that voice before—that voice, or rather one different, but yet very like it.

Downstairs, after a few civil speeches about the pleasure of having the assistance of so great an artistic authority, and sundry contradictory suggestions about styles of furniture and architecture, Greenleaf's host and hostess requested him to join in a little game devised for the removal of precedence in the arrangement of places at table. The game, which had been suggested that very moment by one of the various tall, blond and moustached youths hanging about the drawing-room, consisted in hiding all the men behind a door curtain, whence projected, as sole clue to their identity, their more or less tell-tale feet, by which the ladies were to choose their partners. The feet, so Greenleaf said to himself, were singularly without identity; he saw in his mind's eye the row of projecting, pointed-toed, shining pumps, cut low upon the fantastic assortment of striped, speckled, and otherwise enlivened silk stockings. Among them all there could only be a single pair betraying the nature of their owner, and it was his. They said, or would say, in the mute but expressive language of their square-toedness (Greenleaf felt as if they might have elastic sides even, although his democratic views had always stopped short before that), that their owner was the curate, the tutor, the house-decorator, in fine, the interloper. He wondered whether, as good nature to himself and consideration for the other guests must prompt, those feet would be immediately selected by the mistress of the house, or whether they would be left there unclaimed, when all the others had marched cheerfully off.

But his suspense was quickly converted into another feeling, when among the laughter and exclamations provoked by the performance, a voice came from beyond the curtain, saying slowly: "I think I'll have this pair." The voice was the same he had heard from the lawn, the same he had heard years ago in the British Museum, and on the banks of the Tweed—the same which once or twice since, but at ever-increasing intervals, he had tried in vain to recall to his mind's hearing. The voice—but grown deeper, more deliberate and uniformly weary—of Val Flodden.

Greenleaf heard vaguely the introductory interchange of names performed by his hostess; and felt in his back the well-bred smile of amusement of the couples still behind, as the lady took his unprepared arm and walked him off in the helter-skelter move to the dining-room; and it was as in a dream that he heard his name pronounced, with the added information, on the part of his companion, that it was a long time since they had last met.

"Yes," answered Greenleaf, as the servant gently pushed him and his chair nearer the table; "it must be quite a lot of years ago. I have come here," he added, he scarce knew why—but with a vague sense of protest and self-defence—"about doing up the house."

"Yes, to be sure—it is all going to be overhauled and made beautiful and inappropriate," replied the lady, with a faint intonation of insolence, Greenleaf thought, in her bored voice.

"It is not always easy, is it," rejoined Greenleaf, "to make things appropriate?"

"And beautiful? I suppose not. We aren't any of us very appropriate to a river-bank, with cows lowing and scythes being whetted and all that sort of thing, when one comes to think of it."

"Oh, I do think cows are such interesting creatures—don't you?" put in the charming voice of a charming, charmingly dressed, innocent looking woman opposite, who was evidently the accredited fool of the party. "Sir Robert took us to see a lot of his—all over the dairies, you know—this afternoon, while you were punting."

Another lady, also very charming and charmingly dressed, but neither innocent nor foolish, made some comment on this speech to the man next to her; he said something in his turn, there was a general suppressed laugh, and the innocent looking lady laughed too; but protesting they oughtn't to say such things.

Greenleaf's mind, little accustomed to the charms of innuendoes and slippery allusions, had not followed the intricacies of the conversation. An astonishing girl, beautiful with the beauty of a well-bred horse, sat next to him, and tried to perplex him with sundry questions which she knew he could not follow; but she speedily found there was no rise to be got out of him, and bestowed elsewhere her remarks, racy in more senses than one. So Greenleaf sat silent, looking vaguely at the pools of light beneath the candle-shades, in which the rose petals strewn about, the roses lying loosely, took warm old ivory tints, and the silver—the fantastic confusion of chased salt-cellars and menu-holders and spoons and indescribable objects—flashed blue and lilac on its smooth or chiselled surfaces. From the table the concentrated, shaded light led upwards to the opal necklace of the lady opposite, the blue of the opals changing, with the movement of her head, to green, burning and flickering into fiery sparks; then Greenleaf noticed, sometimes modelled into roundness and sometimes blurred into flatness in the shadow, the black sleeves of the men, the arms of the women, ivory like the rose petals where they advanced beneath the candle-shades; and behind, to the back of the shimmer of the light stuffs and the glare of white shirt-fronts, the big footmen, vague, shadowy, moving about. A man opposite, with babyish eyes and complexion, was telling some story about walking from a punt into the water, which raised the wrath of the girl near Greenleaf; others added further details, which she laughingly tried to deny; there was something about having fastened her garter with a diamond star, and the river having to be dragged for it. Another man, gaunt and languid, said something about not hiding old damask under rose-leaves; but being unnoticed by his hostess, went on about "Parsifal" to his neighbour, the lady interested in cows. There were also allusions to the other Cowes, the place, and to yachting; and a great many to various kinds of sport and to gambling and losing money; indeed, it was marvellous how much money was lost and bankruptcy sustained (technically called *getting broke*).

The men were mostly more good-looking than not; the women, it seemed to Greenleaf, beautiful enough, each of them, to reward a good month's search. There was a smell, cool and white and acute, of gardenias, from the buttonholes, and a warmer, vaguer one of rose petals; the mixture of black coats and indescribable coloured silk, and of bare arms and necks, the alternations of concentrated light and vague shadow, the occasional glint and glimmer of stones, particularly that warm ivory of roses among the silver, struck Greenleaf, long unaccustomed to even much slighter luxury, as extraordinarily beautiful, like some Tadema picture of Roman orgies. And the more beautiful it seemed to him, with its intentional, elaborate beauty, the more did it make him gnash his teeth with the sense of its wickedness, and force him, for his own conscience' sake, to conjure up other pictures: of grimy, gaslit London streets, and battered crowds round barrows of cheap, half-spoilt food.

The lady who had once been called Val Flodden, and whose name—and he fancied he had heard it before—was now Mrs. Hermann Struwë, addressed him with the necessary politeness, and asked him one or two questions about his work and so forth, in a conventional, bored tone. But, although the knowledge that this was his old acquaintance, and the recognition, every now and then, of the fact, put his feelings into a superficial flutter, Greenleaf's mind kept revolving the fact that this woman was really quite a stranger to him; and the apparently somewhat contradictory fact that this was what, after all, he had known she would end in. He noted that among these beautiful and self-satisfied women, with their occasional cleverness and frequent unseemliness of word and allusion, the former Val Flodden was in a way conspicuous, not because she was better looking, but because she was more weary, more reckless, because one somehow expected her to do more, for good or bad, than the others.

"I don't see exactly which of the party could have reported the case," said the woman with the opals, "at least, the crucifix could scarcely have done so … well, well."

There was a great deal of laughter, as the hostess gave the signal for rising; but over it and the rustle and crackle of the ladies' frocks, the voice of Mrs. Hermann Struwë was heard to say in languid, contemptuous tone: "I think your story is a little bit beastly, my dear Algy."

Fortunately for Greenleaf, the men did not stay long at table, as smoking was equally allowed all over the house and in the ladies' presence. For Greenleaf, whose conversation with other men had for years turned only on politics, philosophy, or business, was imbued, much as a woman might have been, with a foregone conviction that as soon as idle men were left to themselves they began to discuss womankind. And there was at the table one man in particular, a long, black, nervous man, with a smiling, jerky mouth, an odd sample of Jewry acclimatised in England, a horrid, half-handsome man, with extraordinarily bland manners and an extraordinarily hard expression, obstinate and mocking, about whom Greenleaf felt that he positively could not sit out any of *his* conversation on women, and, of course, *his* conversation *would* turn on women; partly, perhaps, because the fellow had been introduced as Mr. Hermann Struwë.

Her husband—*that* was her husband! Greenleaf kept repeating to himself, as he answered as best he could his host's remarks about Elizabethan as against Queen Anne. It was only now when he thought of her in connection with this man that Greenleaf realised that he was really a little upset by this meeting with his old acquaintance. And the thought went on and on, round and round, in his head, when he had followed the first stragglers who went to smoke their cigarettes with the ladies, and answered the interrogations of the æsthetic man who had talked about old damask and Wagner. The man in question, delighted to lay hold of so great an authority as Greenleaf, had also noticed that Greenleaf had known Mrs. Hermann Struwë at some former period. He had evidently been snubbed a little by the lady, and partly from a desire to hear her artistic capacities pooh-poohed by a professional (since every amateur imagines himself the only tolerable one), and partly from a natural taste for knowing what did not concern him, he had set very artfully to pump poor Greenleaf, who, at best, was no match for a wily man of the world.

"Miss Flodden had a good deal of talent—quite a remarkable talent—as a draughtsman, had she only studied seriously," he answered emphatically, seeing only that the fellow wished for some quotable piece of running down. "It is, in fact, a pity"—but he stopped. He was really not thinking of that. The long drawing-room opened with all its windows on to the lawn, and you could see, at the bottom of that, the outlines of trees and boats in the moonlight, and Chinese lanterns hanging about the flotilla of moored punts and canoes and skiffs, to which some of the party had gone down, revealing themselves with occasional splashings, thrummings on the banjo, and little cries and peals of laughter. Nearer the house a couple was walking up and down on the grass, the light of the drawing-room lamps catching their faces with an odd, yellow glow every now and then, and making the woman's white frock shimmer like silver against the branches of the big cedars. "It appears Lady Lilly told her mother she was going to try on a frock, but somehow on the way there she met Morton's coach, so she thought she'd get on to it and have some change of air and she changed the air so often that by the evening she had contrived to win sixty pounds at Sandown," said one of the promenading couples, pausing in the stream of light from the window. "Oh, bless your soul, she doesn't mind it's being told; she thinks it an awful joke, and so it was."

That man—that Val Flodden should have married that man—Greenleaf kept repeating to himself, and the recollection of her words about never getting married, about a world where there would be no diamonds and no stepping horses, and also, as she expressed it, no marrying and giving in marriage, filled Greenleaf's mind as with some bitter, heady dram. And he had thought of her as a sort of unapproachable proud amazon, or Diana of

Hippolytus, incapable of any feeling save indignation against injustice and pity for weak and gentle things. Oh Lord, oh Lord! It was horrible, horrible, and at the same time laughable. And just that man, too—that narrow, obstinate looking creature with the brain and the heart (Greenleaf knew it for a certainty) of a barn-door cock! And yet, was he any worse than the others, the others who, perhaps, had a little more brains and a little more heart, and who all the same lived only to waste the work of the poor, to make debts, to gamble, to ruin women, and to fill the world with filthy talk and disbelief in better things? Was he worse than all the other manly, well-mannered, accomplished, futile, or mischievous creatures? Was he worse than *she*?

"Ah, well, of course; you have known her so much more than I have," said the æsthetic man, puffing at his cigarette, opposite to Greenleaf. "But now, I should have thought there would have always been something lacking in anything that woman would do. A certain—I don't know what to call it—but, in short, proper mental balance and steadiness. I consider, that for real artistic quality, it is necessary that one should possess some sort of seriousness, of consistency of character—of course you know her so much better, Mr. Greenleaf—but now I can't understand a really artistic woman—after refusing half a dozen other fellows who were at least gentlemen, suddenly choosing a tubbed Jew like that—and apparently not seeing that he is only a tubbed Jew," the æsthetic man stopped, disappointed in not getting a rise from Greenleaf, but Greenleaf was scarcely listening.

A man had sat down to the piano and was singing, on the whole, rather well. Some of the people were standing by him, others were in little groups, men and women nearly all smoking equally, scattered about the big white room with the delicate blue china, and the big stacks of pale pink begonias. Mrs. Hermann Struwë was standing near the piano, leaning against the long, open window, the principal figure in a group of two other women and a man. In her fanciful, straight-hanging dress of misty-coloured crape, her hair, elaborately and tightly dressed, making her small head even smaller, and her strong, slender neck, with the black pearls around it, drawn up like a peacock's, she struck Greenleaf as much more beautiful than before, and even much taller; but there had been a gentleness, a something timid and winning, in her former occasional little stoop, which was now quite gone. She looked young, but young in quite another way; she was now very thin, and her cheeks were hollowed very perceptibly.

The bland, blurred man at the piano was singing with all his might, and with considerable voice and skill; but the music, of his own composition, was indecorously passionate as he sang it, at least taken in connection with the words, culled from some decadent French poet, and which few people would have deliberately read out aloud. The innocent lady who had talked about cows even made some faint objection, to which the singer answered much surprised, by blandly pointing out the passionate charm of the words, and assuring her that she did not know what real feeling was. And when he had finished that song, and begun another, one of the two other women actually moved away, while the other buried her head in a volume of *Punch*; there was a little murmur, "Well, I think he is going a little too far." But Mrs. Hermann Struwë never moved.

"I can't make out that woman," remarked Greenleaf's new acquaintance, the æsthetic man; "she's usually by ways of being prudish, and has a way of shutting up poor Chatty when he gets into this strain. Only yesterday, she told him his song was beastly, and it wasn't half as bad as this one. I expect she's doing it from cussedness, because her husband was bored at her being too particular yesterday; because, of course, he'll be bored by her not being particular enough to-day."

Greenleaf walked up to a picture, and thence slunk off to the door. As he was leaving the room, he looked back at the former Miss Flodden: she was still standing near the piano, listening composedly, but he thought that her thin face bore an expression of defiance.

He was so excited that he opened his room door too quickly to give effect to a practical joke, consisting of a can of water balancing on its angle as it stood ajar, and intended to tumble on his head while he was passing in; a delicate jest which the girl who had sat next to him—she of the punt, diamond garter and coach adventures—occasionally practised on the new inmates of what she technically called "houses."

IX.

The next morning, after surveying the house with his host, and making elaborate plans for its alteration with his hostess, Greenleaf was going for a stroll outside the grounds, when he suddenly heard his name called by the voice of her who had once been Val Flodden, but of whom he already thought only as Mrs. Hermann Struwë. She arose from under a big cedar, among whose sweeping branches she had been seated reading.

"Are you going for a walk?" she asked, coming towards him in her white frock, incredibly white against the green lawn, and trailing her also incredibly white parasol after her.

"Is it true that you go back to town this afternoon?"

"Yes," answered Greenleaf, laconically.

"Then," she said, "I will come with you a little way."

They walked silently through a little wood of beeches, and out into the meadows by the river. Greenleaf found it too difficult to say anything, and, after all, why say anything to her?

"Look here," began Mrs. Hermann Struwë, suddenly stopping short by the water's brink. "I want to speak to you quite plainly, Mr. Greenleaf. Quite plainly, as one does, don't you know, to a person one isn't likely ever to meet again. I didn't want to speak to you yesterday, because—well—because I disliked you too much."

Greenleaf looked up from the grasses steeping at the root of a big willow, in the water.

"Why?" he asked blankly, but a vague pain invading his consciousness, with the recollection of the library at Yetholme, of the catalogue and the dusty majolica, when Miss Flodden had said once before that she disliked him, because he was taking away the pots.

"But I've thought over it," she went on, not noticing his interruption; "and I see again, what I recognised years ago—only that every now and then I can't help forgetting it and feeling bad—namely, that it was quite natural on your part—I mean your never having introduced me to the Miss Carpenters, nor even written to me again." She spoke slowly and very gently, with just a little hesitation, as he remembered so well her having done those years ago in Northumberland.

An unknown feeling overwhelmed Greenleaf and prevented his speaking— the feeling, he vaguely understood, of having destroyed, of having killed something.

"I don't reproach you with it. I never really did. I understood very soon that it was quite natural on your part to take me for a Princess Casamassima. I had done nothing to make you really know me, and I had no right to expect you to take me on my own telling. And there must have been so many things to make you suspect my not deserving to know your friends, or to learn about your ideas. It wasn't that," she added, hurriedly, "that I wished really to explain, because, as I repeat, although I sometimes feel unreasonable and angry, like last night, when something suddenly makes me see the contrast between what I might have been, and what I am, I don't bear you any grudge. What I wanted to tell you, Mr. Greenleaf, is that I wasn't unworthy of the confidence, though it wasn't much, which you once placed in me. I was not a Princess Casamassima; I was not a humbug then, saying things and getting you to say them for the sake of the novelty. And I'm not really changed since. I wasn't a worthless woman then; and I haven't really become a worthless woman now. Shall we go towards home? I think I heard the gong."

They were skirting the full river, with its fringe of steeping loose-strife and meadow-sweet, and its clumps of sedge, starred with forget-me-not, whence whirred occasional water-fowl. From the field opposite there came every now and then the lazy low of a cow.

"It was very different, wasn't it, on the Tweed," she said, looking round her; "the banks so steep and bare, and all that shingle. Do you remember the heron? Didn't he look Japanese? I hate all this," and she dug up a pellet of green with her parasol point, and flung it far into the water.

"Of course," she went on, "to you it must seem the very proof of your suspicions having been justified, I mean your finding me again—well, in this house. And, perhaps, you may remember my telling you, all those years ago at Yetholme, that I would never marry."

She raised her eyes from the ground and looked straight into his, with that odd deepening of colour of her own. She had guessed his thoughts: that sentence about not marrying and being given in marriage was ringing in his mind; and he felt, as she looked into his face, that she wished above all to clear herself from that unspoken accusation.

"I never should have, most likely," she went on. "Although you must remember that all my bringing up had consisted in teaching me that a woman's one business in life *is* to marry, to make a good marriage, to marry into this set, a man like my husband. For a long while before I ever met you, I had made up my mind that although this was undoubtedly the natural and virtuous course, I would not follow it, that I would rather earn my living or starve; and I had been taught that to do either, to go one's own ways and think one's own thoughts, was scandalous. It was about this that I had broken with my sister. She had bothered me to marry one of a variety of men whom she unearthed for the purpose; and we quarrelled because I refused the one she wanted me to have most—the one, as a matter of fact, who is now my husband. I tell you all these uninteresting things because I want you to know that I was in earnest when I told you I did not want the things a woman gets by marrying. I was in earnest," she went on, stopping and twisting a long willow leaf round her finger, the tone of her voice changing suddenly from almost defiant earnestness to a sad, helpless little tone, "but it was of no good. I saw—you showed me—that I was locked, walled into the place into which I had been born; you made me feel that it was useless for an outsider to try to gain the confidence of you people who work and care about things; that your friends would consider me an intruder, that you considered me a humbug—you slammed in my face the little door through which I had hoped to have escaped from all this sort of thing."

And she nodded towards the white house, stretched like a little encampment upon the green river bank, with the flotilla of boats and punts and steam launches, moored before its windows.

"Then," said Greenleaf, a light coming into his mind, a light such as would reveal some great ruin of flood or fire to the unconscious criminal who has opened the sluice or dropped the match in the dark, "then you sat out that song last night to make me understand...?"

"It was very childish of me, and also very unjust," answered Mrs. Hermann composedly. "Of course you couldn't help it. I don't feel angry with you. But sometimes, when I remember those weeks when I gradually understood that it was all to be, and I made up my mind to live out the life for which I had been born—and, now that the pots were sold—well, to sell myself also to the highest bidder—sometimes I did feel a little bad. You see when one is really honest oneself, it is hard to be misunderstood—and the more misunderstood the more one explains oneself—by other people who are honest."

They walked along in silence; which Greenleaf broke by asking as in a dream—"And your violin?"

"Oh! I've given that up long ago—my husband didn't like it, and as he has given me everything that I possess, it wouldn't be business, would it, to do things he dislikes? If it had been the piano, or the guitar, or the banjo! But a woman can't lock herself up and practice the fiddle! People would think it odd. And now," she added, as they came in sight of the little groups of variegated pink and mauve frocks, and the white boating-clothes under the big cedars, "good-bye, Mr. Greenleaf; and—be a little more trustful to other people who may want your friendship—won't you? I shall like to think of that." She stretched out her hand, with the thin glove loosely wrinkled over the arm, and she smiled that good, wide-eyed smile, like that of a good, serious child who wishes to understand.

Greenleaf did not take her hand at once.

"You have children at least?" he asked hoarsely.

She understood his thought, but hesitated before answering.

"I have three—somewhere—at the sea-side, or some other place where children ought to be when their parents go staying about,"—she answered quickly—"they are quite happy, with plenty of toys, now; and they will be quite happy when they grow up, for they will have plenty of money, and they will be their father's image—good-bye!"

"Good-bye," answered Greenleaf, and added, after he had let go her hand, "It is very generous of you to be so forgiving. But your generosity makes it only more impossible for me ever to forgive myself."

Out of the station of that little group of river houses the line goes almost immediately on to a long bridge. It was in process of repair, and as the train moved slowly across, Greenleaf could see, on the upper river reach, close beneath him, a flotilla of boats, canoes, and skiffs of various sizes, surrounding a punt, and all of them gay with lilac and pale green and pale pink frocks, and white flannels, and coloured sashes and cushions, and fantastic umbrellas. Some of the ladies were scrambling from one of the skiffs into the punt, which was pinned into its place by the long pole held upright in the green, glassy water, reflecting the pink, green, lilac, and white, the red cushions, and the shimmering greyness of the big willows. There was much laughter and some little shrieks, and the twang of a banjo; and it looked altogether like some modern Watteau's version of a latter-day embarkation for the island of Venus. And, in the little heap of bright colours, Greenleaf recognised, over the side of a skiff, the parasol, white, incredibly white, of the former Val Flodden.

THE LEGEND OF MADAME KRASINSKA.

It is a necessary part of this story to explain how I have come by it, or rather, how it has chanced to have me for its writer.

I was very much impressed one day by a certain nun of the order calling themselves Little Sisters of the Poor. I had been taken to these sisters to support the recommendation of a certain old lady, the former door-keeper of his studio, whom my friend Cecco Bandini wished to place in the asylum. It turned out, of course, that Cecchino was perfectly able to plead his case without my assistance; so I left him blandishing the Mother Superior in the big, cheerful kitchen, and begged to be shown over the rest of the establishment. The sister who was told off to accompany me was the one of whom I would speak.

This lady was tall and slight; her figure, as she preceded me up the narrow stairs and through the whitewashed wards, was uncommonly elegant and charming; and she had a girlish rapidity of movement, which caused me to experience a little shock at the first real sight which I caught of her face. It was young and remarkably pretty, with a kind of refinement peculiar to American women; but it was inexpressibly, solemnly tragic; and one felt that under her tight linen cap, the hair must be snow white. The tragedy, whatever it might have been, was now over; and the lady's expression, as she spoke to the old creatures scraping the ground in the garden, ironing the sheets in the laundry, or merely huddling over their braziers in the chill winter sunshine, was pathetic only by virtue of its strange present tenderness, and by that trace of terrible past suffering.

She answered my questions very briefly, and was as taciturn as ladies of religious communities are usually loquacious. Only, when I expressed my admiration for the institution which contrived to feed scores of old paupers on broken victuals begged from private houses and inns, she turned her eyes full upon me and said, with an earnestness which was almost passionate, "Ah, the old! The old! It is so much, much worse for them than for any others. Have you ever tried to imagine what it is to be poor and forsaken and old?"

These words and the strange ring in the sister's voice, the strange light in her eyes, remained in my memory. What was not, therefore, my surprise when, on returning to the kitchen, I saw her start and lay hold of the back of the chair as soon as she caught sight of Cecco Bandini. Cecco, on his side also, was visibly startled, but only after a moment; it was clear that she recognised him long before he identified her. What little romance could there exist in common between my eccentric painter and that serene but tragic Sister of the Poor?

A week later, it became evident that Cecco Bandini had come to explain the mystery; but to explain it (as I judged by the embarrassment of his manner) by one of those astonishingly elaborate lies occasionally attempted by perfectly frank persons. It was not the case. Cecchino had come indeed to explain that little dumb scene which had passed between him and the Little Sister of the Poor. He had come, however, not to satisfy my curiosity, or to overcome my suspicions, but to execute a commission which he had greatly at heart; to help, as he expressed it, in the accomplishment of a good work by a real saint.

Of course, he explained, smiling that good smile under his black eyebrows and white moustache, he did not expect me to believe very literally the story which he had undertaken to get me to write. He only asked, and the lady only wished, me, to write down her narrative without any comments, and leave to the heart of the reader the decision about its truth or falsehood.

For this reason, and the better to attain the object of appealing to the profane, rather than to the religious, reader, I have abandoned the order of narrative of the Little Sister of the Poor; and attempted to turn her pious legend into a worldly story, as follows:—

I.

Cecco Bandini had just returned from the Maremma, to whose solitary marshes and jungles he had fled in one of his fits of fury at the stupidity and wickedness of the civilised world. A great many months spent among buffaloes and wild boars, conversing only with those wild cherry-trees, of whom he used whimsically to say, "they are such good little folk," had sent him back with an extraordinary zest for civilisation, and a comic tendency to find its products, human and otherwise, extraordinary, picturesque, and suggestive. He was in this frame of mind when there came a light rap on his door-slate; and two ladies appeared on the threshold of his studio, with the shaven face and cockaded hat of a tall footman over-topping them from behind. One of them was unknown to our painter; the other was numbered among Cecchino's very few grand acquaintances.

"Why haven't you been round to me yet, you savage?" she asked, advancing quickly with a brusque hand-shake and a brusque bright gleam of eyes and teeth, well-bred but audacious and a trifle ferocious. And dropping on to a divan she added, nodding first at her companion and then at the pictures all round, "I have brought my friend, Madame Krasinska, to see your things," and she began poking with her parasol at the contents of a gaping portfolio.

The Baroness Fosca—for such was her name—was one of the cleverest and fastest ladies of the place, with a taste for art and ferociously frank conversation. To Cecco Bandini, as she lay back among her furs on that shabby divan of his, she appeared in the light of the modern Lucretia Borgia, the tamed panther of fashionable life. "What an interesting thing civilisation is!" he thought, watching her every movement with the eyes of the imagination; "why, you might spend years among the wild folk of the Maremma without meeting such a tremendous, terrible, picturesque, powerful creature as this!"

Cecchino was so absorbed in the Baroness Fosca, who was in reality not at all a Lucretia Borgia, but merely an impatient lady bent upon amusing and being amused, that he was scarcely conscious of the presence of her companion. He knew that she was very young, very pretty, and very smart, and that he had made her his best bow, and offered her his least rickety chair; for the rest, he sat opposite to his Lucretia Borgia of modern life, who had meanwhile found a cigarette, and was puffing away and explaining that she was about to give a fancy ball, which should be the most *crâne*, the only amusing thing, of the year.

"Oh," he exclaimed, kindling at the thought, "do let me design you a dress all black and white and wicked green—you shall go as Deadly Nightshade, as Belladonna Atropa——;"

"Belladonna Atropa! why my ball is in comic costume" ... The Baroness was answering contemptuously, when Cecchino's attention was suddenly called to the other end of the studio by an exclamation on the part of his other visitor.

"Do tell me all about her;—has she a name? Is she really a lunatic?" asked the young lady who had been introduced as Madame Krasinska, keeping a portfolio open with one hand, and holding up in the other a coloured sketch she had taken from it.

"What have you got there? Oh, only the Sora Lena!" and Madame Fosca reverted to the contemplation of the smoke-rings she was making.

"Tell me about her—Sora Lena, did you say?" asked the younger lady eagerly.

She spoke French, but with a pretty little American accent, despite her Polish name. She was very charming, Cecchino said to himself, a radiant impersonation of youthful brightness and elegance as she stood there in her long, silvery furs, holding the drawing with tiny, tight-gloved hands, and shedding around her a vague, exquisite fragrance—no, not a mere literal perfume, that would be far too coarse but something personal akin to it.

"I have noticed her so often," she went on, with that silvery young voice of hers; "she's mad, isn't she? And what did you say her name was? Please tell me again."

Cecchino was delighted. "How true it is," he reflected, "that only refinement, high-breeding, luxury can give people certain kinds of sensitiveness, of rapid intuition! No woman of another class would have picked out just that drawing, or would have been interested in it without stupid laughter."

"Do you want to know the story of poor old Sora Lena?" asked Cecchino, taking the sketch from Madame Krasinska's hand, and looking over it at the charming, eager young face.

The sketch might have passed for a caricature; but anyone who had spent so little as a week in Florence those six or seven years ago would have recognised at once that it was merely a faithful portrait. For Sora Lena—more correctly Signora Maddalena—had been for years and years one of the most conspicuous sights of the town. In all weathers you might have seen that hulking old woman, with her vague, staring, reddish face, trudging through the streets or standing before shops, in her extraordinary costume of thirty years ago, her enormous crinoline, on which the silk skirt and ragged petticoat hung limply, her gigantic coal-scuttle bonnet, shawl, prunella boots, and great muff or parasol; one of several outfits, all alike, of that distant period, all alike inexpressibly dirty and tattered. In all weathers you might have seen her stolidly going her way, indifferent to stares and jibes, of which, indeed, there were by this time comparatively few, so familiar had she grown to staring, jibing Florence. In all weathers, but most noticeably in the worst, as if the squalor of mud and rain had an affinity with that sad, draggled, soiled, battered piece of human squalor, that lamentable rag of half-witted misery.

"Do you want to know about Sora Lena?" repeated Cecco Bandini, meditatively. They formed a strange, strange contrast, these two women, the one in the sketch and the one standing before him. And there was to him a pathetic whimsicalness in the interest which the one had excited in the other. "How long has she been wandering about here? Why, as long as I can remember the streets of Florence, and that," added Cecchino sorrowfully, "is a longer while than I care to count up. It seems to me as if she must always have been there, like the olive-trees and the paving stones; for after all, Giotto's tower was not there before Giotto, whereas poor old Sora Lena— But, by the way, there is a limit even to her. There is a legend about her; they say that she was once sane, and had two sons, who went as Volunteers in '59, and were killed at Solferino, and ever since then she has sallied forth, every day, winter or summer, in her best clothes, to meet the young fellows at the Station. May be. To my mind it doesn't matter much whether the story be true or false; it is fitting," and Cecco Bandini set about dusting some canvases which had attracted the Baroness Fosca's attention. When Cecchino was helping that lady into her furs, she gave one of her little brutal smiles, and nodded in the direction of her companion.

"Madame Krasinska," she said laughing, "is very desirous of possessing one of your sketches, but she is too polite to ask you the price of it. That's what comes of our not knowing how to earn a penny for ourselves, doesn't it, Signor Cecchino?"

Madame Krasinska blushed, and looked more young, and delicate, and charming.

"I did not know whether you would consent to part with one of your drawings," she said in her silvery, child-like voice,—"it is—this one—which I should so much have liked to have— ... to have ... bought." Cecchino smiled at the embarrassment which the word "bought" produced in his exquisite visitor. Poor, charming young creature, he thought; the only thing she thinks people one knows can sell, is themselves, and that's called getting married. "You must explain to your friend," said Cecchino to the Baroness Fosca, as he hunted in a drawer for a piece of clean paper, "that such rubbish as this is neither bought nor sold; it is not even possible for a poor devil of a painter to offer it as a gift to a lady—but,"—and he handed the little roll to Madame Krasinska, making his very best bow as he did so—"it is possible for a lady graciously to accept it."

"Thank you so much," answered Madame Krasinska, slipping the drawing into her muff; "it is very good of you to give me such a ... such a very interesting sketch," and she pressed his big, brown fingers in her little grey-gloved hand.

"Poor Sora Lena!" exclaimed Cecchino, when there remained of the visit only a faint perfume of exquisiteness; and he thought of the hideous old draggle-tailed mad woman, reposing, rolled up in effigy, in the delicious daintiness of that delicate grey muff.

II.

A fortnight later, the great event was Madame Fosca's fancy ball, to which the guests were bidden to come in what was described as comic costume. Some, however, craved leave to appear in their ordinary apparel, and among these was Cecchino Bandini, who was persuaded, moreover, that his old-fashioned swallow-tails, which he donned only at weddings, constituted quite comic costume enough.

This knowledge did not interfere at all with his enjoyment. There was even, to his whimsical mind, a certain charm in being in a crowd among which he knew no one; unnoticed or confused, perhaps, with the waiters, as he hung about the stairs and strolled through the big palace rooms. It was as good as wearing an invisible cloak, one saw so much just because one was not seen; indeed, one was momentarily endowed (it seemed at least to his fanciful apprehension) with a faculty akin to that of understanding the talk of birds; and, as he watched and listened he became aware of innumerable charming little romances, which were concealed from more notable but less privileged persons.

Little by little the big white and gold rooms began to fill. The ladies, who had moved in gorgeous isolation, their skirts displayed as finely as a peacock's train, became gradually visible only from the waist upwards; and only the branches of the palm-trees and tree ferns detached themselves against the shining walls. Instead of wandering among variegated brocades and iridescent silks and astonishing arrangements of feathers and flowers, Cecchino's eye was forced to a higher level by the thickening crowd; it was now the constellated sparkle of diamonds on neck and head which dazzled him, and the strange, unaccustomed splendour of white arms and shoulders. And, as the room filled, the invisible cloak was also drawn closer round our friend Cecchino, and the extraordinary faculty of perceiving romantic and delicious secrets in other folk's bosoms became more and more developed. They seemed to him like exquisite children, these creatures rustling about in fantastic dresses, powdered shepherds and shepherdesses with diamonds spirting fire among their ribbons and top-knots; Japanese and Chinese embroidered with sprays of flowers; mediæval and antique beings, and beings hidden in the plumage of birds, or the petals of flowers; children, but children somehow matured, transfigured by the touch of luxury and good-breeding, children full of courtesy and kindness. There were, of course, a few costumes which might have been better conceived or better carried out, or better— not to say best—omitted altogether. One grew bored, after a little while, with people dressed as marionettes, champagne bottles, sticks of sealing-wax, or captive balloons; a young man arrayed as a female ballet dancer, and another got up as a wet nurse, with baby *obligato* might certainly have been dispensed with. Also, Cecchino could not help wincing a little at the daughter of the house being mummed and painted to represent her own grandmother, a respectable old lady whose picture hung in the dining-room, and whose spectacles he had frequently picked up in his boyhood. But these were mere trifling details. And, as a whole, it was beautiful, fantastic. So Cecchino moved backward and forward, invisible in his shabby black suit, and borne hither and thither by the well-bred pressure of the many-coloured crowd; pleasantly blinded by the innumerable lights, the sparkle of chandelier pendants, and the shooting flames of jewels; gently deafened by the confused murmur of innumerable voices, of crackling stuffs and soughing fans, of distant dance music; and inhaling the vague fragrance which seemed less the decoction of cunning perfumers than the exquisite and expressive emanation of this exquisite bloom of personality. Certainly, he said to himself, there is no pleasure so delicious as seeing people amusing themselves with refinement: there is a transfiguring magic, almost a moralising power, in wealth and elegance and good-breeding.

He was making this reflection, and watching between two dances, a tiny fluff of down sailing through the warm draught across the empty space, the sort of whirlpool of the ball-room—when a little burst of voices came from the entrance saloon. The multi-coloured costumes fluttered like butterflies toward a given spot, there was a little heaping together of brilliant colours and flashing jewels. There was much craning of delicate, fluffy young necks and heads, and shuffle on tiptoe, and the crowd fell automatically aside. A little gangway was cleared; and there walked into the middle of the white and gold drawing-room, a lumbering, hideous figure, with reddish, vacant face, sunk in an immense, tarnished satin bonnet; and draggled, faded, lilac silk skirts spread over a vast dislocated crinoline. The feet dabbed along in the broken prunella boots; the mangy rabbit-skin muff bobbed loosely with the shambling gait; and then, under the big chandelier, there came a sudden pause, and the thing looked slowly round, a gaping, mooning, blear-eyed stare.

It was the Sora Lena.

There was a perfect storm of applause.

III.

Cecchino Bandini did not slacken his pace till he found himself, with his thin overcoat and opera hat all drenched, among the gas reflections and puddles before his studio door; that shout of applause and that burst of clapping pursuing him down the stairs of the palace and all through the rainy streets. There were a few embers in his stove; he threw a faggot on them, lit a cigarette, and proceeded to make reflections, the wet opera hat still on his head. He had been a fool, a savage. He had behaved like a child, rushing past his hostess with that ridiculous speech in answer to her inquiries: "I am running away because bad luck has entered your house."

Why had he not guessed it at once? What on earth else could she have wanted his sketch for?

He determined to forget the matter, and, as he imagined, he forgot it. Only, when the next day's evening paper displayed two columns describing Madame Fosca's ball, and more particularly "that mask," as the reporter had it, "which among so many which were graceful and ingenious, bore off in triumph the palm for witty novelty," he threw the paper down and gave it a kick towards the wood-box. But he felt ashamed of himself, picked it up, smoothed it out and read it all—foreign news and home news, and even the description of Madame Fosca's masked ball, conscientiously through. Last of all he perused, with dogged resolution, the column of petty casualties: a boy bit in the calf by a dog who was not mad; the frustrated burgling of a baker's shop; even to the bunches of keys and the umbrella and two cigar-cases picked up by the police, and consigned to the appropriate municipal limbo; until he came to the following lines: "This morning the *Guardians of Public Safety*, having been called by the neighbouring inhabitants, penetrated into a room on the top floor of a house situate in the Little Street of the Gravedigger (Viccolo del Beccamorto), and discovered, hanging from a rafter, the dead body of Maddalena X. Y. Z. The deceased had long been noted throughout Florence for her eccentric habits and apparel." The paragraph was headed, in somewhat larger type: "Suicide of a female lunatic."

Cecchino's cigarette had gone out, but he continued blowing at it all the same. He could see in his mind's eye a tall, slender figure, draped in silvery plush and silvery furs, standing by the side of an open portfolio, and holding a drawing in her tiny hand, with the slender, solitary gold bangle over the grey glove.

IV.

Madame Krasinska was in a very bad humour. The old Chanoiness, her late husband's aunt, noticed it; her guests noticed it; her maid noticed it: and she noticed it herself. For, of all human beings, Madame Krasinska—Netta, as smart folk familiarly called her—was the least subject to bad humour. She was as uniformly cheerful as birds are supposed to be, and she certainly had none of the causes for anxiety or sorrow which even the most proverbial bird must occasionally have. She had always had money, health, good looks; and people had always told her—in New York, in London, in Paris, Rome, and St. Petersburg—from her very earliest childhood, that her one business in life was to amuse herself. The old gentleman whom she had simply and cheerfully accepted as a husband, because he had given her quantities of bonbons, and was going to give her quantities of diamonds, had been kind, and had been kindest of all in dying of sudden bronchitis when away for a month, leaving his young widow with an affectionately indifferent recollection of him, no remorse of any kind, and a great deal of money, not to speak of the excellent Chanoiness, who constituted an invaluable chaperon. And, since his happy demise, no cloud had disturbed the cheerful life or feelings of Madame Krasinska. Other women, she knew, had innumerable subjects of wretchedness; or if they had none, they were wretched from the want of them. Some had children who made them unhappy, others were unhappy for lack of children, and similarly as to lovers; but she had never had a child and never had a lover, and never experienced the smallest desire for either. Other women suffered from sleeplessness, or from sleepiness, and took morphia or abstained from morphia with equal inconvenience; other women also grew weary of amusement. But Madame Krasinska always slept beautifully, and always stayed awake cheerfully; and Madame Krasinska was never tired of amusing herself. Perhaps it was all this which culminated in the fact that Madame Krasinska had never in all her life envied or disliked anybody; and that no one, apparently, had ever envied or disliked her. She did not wish to outshine or supplant any one; she did not want to be richer, younger, more beautiful, or more adored than they. She only wanted to amuse herself, and she succeeded in so doing.

This particular day—the day after Madame Fosca's ball—Madame Krasinska was not amusing herself. She was not at all tired: she never was; besides, she had remained in bed till mid-day: neither was she unwell, for that also she never was; nor had anyone done the slightest thing to vex her. But there it was. She was not amusing herself at all. She could not tell why; and she could not tell why, also, she was vaguely miserable. When the first batch of afternoon callers had taken leave, and the following batches had been sent away from the door, she threw down her volume of Gyp, and walked to the window. It was raining: a thin, continuous spring drizzle. Only a few cabs, with wet, shining backs, an occasional lumbering omnibus or cart, passed by with wheezing, straining, downcast horses. In one or two shops a light was appearing, looking tiny, blear, and absurd in the gray afternoon. Madame Krasinska looked out for a few minutes; then, suddenly turning round, she brushed past the big palms and azaleas, and rang the bell.

"Order the brougham at once," she said.

She could by no means have explained what earthly reason had impelled her to go out. When the footman had inquired for orders she felt at a loss: certainly she did not want to go to see anyone, nor to buy anything, nor to inquire about anything.

What *did* she want? Madame Krasinska was not in the habit of driving out in the rain for her pleasure; still less to drive out without knowing whither. What did she want? She sat muffled in her furs, looking out on the wet, grey streets as the brougham rolled aimlessly along. She wanted—she wanted—she couldn't tell what. But she wanted it very much. That much she knew very well—she wanted. The rain, the wet streets, the muddy crossings—oh, how dismal they were! and still she wished to go on.

Instinctively, her polite coachman made for the politer streets, for the polite Lung' Arno. The river quay was deserted, and a warm, wet wind swept lazily along its muddy flags. Madame Krasinska let down the glass. How dreary! The foundry, on the other side, let fly a few red sparks from its tall chimney into the grey sky; the water droned over the weir; a lamp-lighter hurried along.

Madame Krasinska pulled the check-string.

"I want to walk," she said.

The polite footman followed behind along the messy flags, muddy and full of pools; the brougham followed behind him. Madame Krasinska was not at all in the habit of walking on the embankment, still less walking in the rain.

After some minutes she got in again, and bade the carriage drive home. When she got into the lit streets she again pulled the check-string and ordered the brougham to proceed at a foot's pace. At a certain spot she remembered something, and bade the coachman draw up before a shop. It was the big chemist's.

"What does the Signora Contessa command?" and the footman raised his hat over his ear. Somehow she had forgotten. "Oh," she answered, "wait a minute. Now I remember, it's the next shop, the florist's. Tell them to send fresh azaleas to-morrow and fetch away the old ones."

Now the azaleas had been changed only that morning. But the polite footman obeyed. And Madame Krasinska remained for a minute, nestled in her fur rug, looking on to the wet, yellow, lit pavement, and into the big chemist's window. There were the red, heart-shaped chest protectors, the frictioning gloves, the bath towels, all hanging in their place. Then boxes of eau-de-Cologne, lots of bottles of all sizes, and boxes, large and small, and variosities of indescribable nature and use, and the great glass jars, yellow, blue, green, and ruby red, with a spark from the gas lamp behind in their heart. She stared at it all, very intently, and without a notion about any of these objects. Only she knew that the glass jars were uncommonly bright, and that each had a ruby, or topaz, or emerald of gigantic size, in its heart. The footman returned.

"Drive home," ordered Madame Krasinska. As her maid was taking her out of her dress, a thought—the first since so long—flashed across her mind, at the sight of certain skirts, and an uncouth cardboard mask, lying in a corner of her dressing-room. How odd that she had not seen the Sora Lena that evening.... She used always to be walking in the lit streets at that hour.

V.

The next morning Madame Krasinska woke up quite cheerful and happy. But she began, nevertheless, to suffer, ever since the day after the Fosca ball, from the return of that quite unprecedented and inexplicable depression. Her days became streaked, as it were, with moments during which it was quite impossible to amuse herself; and these moments grew gradually into hours. People bored her for no accountable reason, and things which she had expected as pleasures brought with them a sense of vague or more distinct wretchedness. Thus she would find herself in the midst of a ball or dinner-party, invaded suddenly by a confused sadness or boding of evil, she did not know which. And once, when a box of new clothes had arrived from Paris, she was overcome, while putting on one of the frocks, with such a fit of tears that she had to be put to bed instead of going to the Tornabuoni's party.

Of course, people began to notice this change; indeed, Madame Krasinska had ingenuously complained of the strange alteration in herself. Some persons suggested that she might be suffering from slow blood-poisoning, and urged an inquiry into the state of the drains. Others recommended arsenic, morphia, or antipyrine. One kind friend brought her a box of peculiar cigarettes; another forwarded a parcel of still more peculiar novels; most people had some pet doctor to cry up to the skies; and one or two suggested her changing her confessor; not to mention an attempt being made to mesmerise her into cheerfulness.

When her back was turned, meanwhile, all the kind friends discussed the probability of an unhappy love affair, loss of money on the Stock Exchange, and similar other explanations. And while one devoted lady tried to worm out of her the name of her unfaithful lover and of the rival for whom he had forsaken her, another assured her that she was suffering from a lack of personal affections. It was a fine opportunity for the display of pietism, materialism, idealism, realism, psychological lore, and esoteric theosophy.

Oddly enough, all this zeal about herself did not worry Madame Krasinska, as she would certainly have expected it to worry any other woman. She took a little of each of the tonic or soporific drugs; and read a little of each of those sickly sentimental, brutal, or politely improper novels. She also let herself be accompanied to various doctors; and she got up early in the morning and stood for an hour on a chair in a crowd in order to benefit by the preaching of the famous Father Agostino. She was quite patient even with the friends who condoled about the lover or absence of such. For all these things became, more and more, completely indifferent to Madame Krasinska—unrealities which had no weight in the presence of the painful reality.

This reality was that she was rapidly losing all power of amusing herself, and that when she did occasionally amuse herself she had to pay for what she called this *good time* by an increase of listlessness and melancholy.

It was not melancholy or listlessness such as other women complained of. They seemed, in their fits of blues, to feel that the world around them had got all wrong, or at least was going out of its way to annoy them. But Madame Krasinska saw the world quite plainly, proceeding in the usual manner, and being quite as good a world as before. It was she who was all wrong. It was, in the literal sense of the words, what she supposed people might mean when they said that So-and-so was *not himself*; only that So-and-so, on examination, appeared to be very much himself—only himself in a worse temper than usual. Whereas she… Why, in her case, she really did not seem to be herself any longer. Once, at a grand dinner, she suddenly ceased eating and talking to her neighbour, and surprised herself wondering who the people all were and what they had come for. Her mind would become, every now and then, a blank; a blank at least full of vague images, misty and muddled, which she was unable to grasp, but of which she knew that they were painful, weighing on her as a heavy load must weigh on the head or back. Something had happened, or was going to happen, she could not remember which, but she burst into tears none the less. In the midst of such a state of things, if visitors or a servant entered, she would ask sometimes who they were. Once a man came to call, during one of these fits; by an effort she was able to receive him and answer his small talk more or less at random, feeling the whole time as if someone else were speaking in her place. The visitor at length rose to depart, and they both stood for a moment in the midst of the drawing-room.

"This is a very pretty house; it must belong to some rich person. Do you know to whom it belongs?" suddenly remarked Madame Krasinska, looking slowly round her at the furniture, the pictures, statuettes, nicknacks, the screens and plants. "Do you know to whom it belongs?" she repeated.

"It belongs to the most charming lady in Florence," stammered out the visitor politely, and fled.

"My darling Netta," exclaimed the Chanoiness from where she was seated crocheting benevolently futile garments by the fire; "you should not joke in that way. That poor young man was placed in a painful, in a very painful position by your nonsense."

Madame Krasinska leaned her arms on a screen, and stared her respectable relation long in the face.

"You seem a kind woman," she said at length. "You are old, but then you aren't poor, and they don't call you a mad woman. That makes all the difference."

Then she set to singing—drumming out the tune on the screen—the soldier song of '59, *Addio, mia bella, addio.*

"Netta!" cried the Chanoiness, dropping one ball of worsted after another. "Netta!"

But Madame Krasinska passed her hand over her brow and heaved a great sigh. Then she took a cigarette off a cloisonné tray, dipped a spill in the fire and remarked,

"Would you like to have the brougham to go to see your friend at the Sacré Cœur, Aunt Thérèse? I have promised to wait in for Molly Wolkonsky and Bice Forteguerra. We are going to dine at *Doney's* with young Pomfret."

VI.

Madame Krasinska had repeated her evening drives in the rain. Indeed she began also to walk about regardless of weather. Her maid asked her whether she had been ordered exercise by the doctor, and she answered yes. But why she should not walk in the Cascine or along the Lung' Arno, and why she should always choose the muddiest thoroughfares, the maid did not inquire. As it was, Madame Krasinska never showed any repugnance or seemly contrition for the state of draggle in which she used to return home; sometimes when the woman was unbuttoning her boots, she would remain in contemplation of their muddiness, murmuring things which Jefferies could not understand. The servants, indeed, declared that the Countess must have gone out of her mind. The footman related that she used to stop the brougham, get out and look into the lit shops, and that he had to stand behind, in order to prevent lady-killing youths of a caddish description from whispering expressions of admiration in her ear. And once, he affirmed with horror, she had stopped in front of a certain cheap eating-house, and looked in at the bundles of asparagus, at the uncooked chops displayed in the window. And then, added the footman, she had turned round to him slowly and said,

"They have good food in there."

And meanwhile, Madame Krasinska went to dinners and parties, and gave them, and organised picnics, as much as was decently possible in Lent, and indeed a great deal more.

She no longer complained of the blues; she assured everyone that she had completely got rid of them, that she had never been in such spirits in all her life. She said it so often, and in so excited a way, that judicious people declared that now that lover must really have jilted her, or gambling on the Stock Exchange have brought her to the verge of ruin.

Nay, Madame Krasinska's spirits became so obstreperous as to change her in sundry ways. Although living in the fastest set, Madame Krasinska had never been a fast woman. There was something childlike in her nature which made her modest and decorous. She had never learned to talk slang, or to take up vulgar attitudes, or to tell impossible stories; and she had never lost a silly habit of blushing at expressions and anecdotes which she did not reprove other women for using and relating. Her amusements had never been flavoured with that spice of impropriety, of curiosity of evil, which was common in her set. She liked putting on pretty frocks, arranging pretty furniture, driving in well got up carriages, eating good dinners, laughing a great deal, and dancing a great deal, and that was all.

But now Madame Krasinska suddenly altered. She became, all of a sudden, anxious for those exotic sensations which honest women may get by studying the ways, and frequenting the haunts, of women by no means honest. She made up parties to go to the low theatres and music-halls; she proposed dressing up and going, in company with sundry adventurous spirits, for evening strolls in the more dubious portions of the town. Moreover, she, who had never touched a card, began to gamble for large sums, and to surprise people by producing a folded green roulette cloth and miniature roulette rakes out of her pocket. And she became so outrageously conspicuous in her flirtations (she who had never flirted before), and so outrageously loud in her manners and remarks, that her good friends began to venture a little remonstrance....

But remonstrance was all in vain; and she would toss her head and laugh cynically, and answer in a brazen, jarring voice.

For Madame Krasinska felt that she must live, live noisily, live scandalously, live her own life of wealth and dissipation, because ...

She used to wake up at night with the horror of that suspicion. And in the middle of the day, pull at her clothes, tear down her hair, and rush to the mirror and stare at herself, and look for every feature, and clutch for every end of silk, or bit of lace, or wisp of hair, which proved that she was really herself. For gradually, slowly, she had come to understand that she was herself no longer.

Herself—well, yes, of course she was herself. Was it not herself who rushed about in such a riot of amusement; herself whose flushed cheeks and over-bright eyes, and cynically flaunted neck and bosom she saw in the glass, whose mocking loud voice and shrill laugh she listened to? Besides, did not her servants, her visitors, know her as Netta Krasinska; and did she not know how to wear her clothes, dance, make jokes, and encourage men, afterwards to discourage them? This, she often said to herself, as she lay awake the long nights, as she sat out the longer nights gambling and chaffing, distinctly proved that she really was herself. And she repeated it all mentally when she returned, muddy, worn out, and as awakened from a ghastly dream, after one of her long rambles through the streets, her daily walks towards the station.

But still.... What of those strange forebodings of evil, those muddled fears of some dreadful calamity ... something which had happened, or was going to happen ... poverty, starvation, death—whose death, her own? or someone else's? That knowledge that it was all, all over; that blinding, felling blow which used every now and then to crush her.... Yes, she had felt that first at the railway station. At the station? but what had happened at the station? Or was it going to happen still? Since to the station her feet seemed unconsciously to carry her every day. What was it all? Ah! she knew. There was a woman, an old woman, walking to the station to meet.... Yes, to meet a regiment on its way back. They came back, those soldiers, among a mob yelling triumph. She remembered the illuminations, the red, green, and white lanterns, and those garlands all over the waiting-rooms. And quantities of flags. The bands played. So gaily! They played Garibaldi's hymn, and *Addio, Mia Bella*. Those pieces always made her cry now. The station was crammed, and all the boys, in tattered, soiled uniforms, rushed into the arms of parents, wives, friends. Then there was like a blinding light, a crash... An officer led the old woman gently out of the place, mopping his eyes. And she, of all the crowd, was the only one to go home alone. Had it really all happened? and to whom? Had it really happened to her, had her boys.... But Madame Krasinska had never had any boys.

It was dreadful how much it rained in Florence; and stuff boots do wear out so quick in mud. There was such a lot of mud on the way to the station; but of course it was necessary to go to the station in order to meet the train from Lombardy—the boys must be met.

There was a place on the other side of the river where you went in and handed your watch and your brooch over the counter, and they gave you some money and a paper. Once the paper got lost. Then there was a mattress, too. But there was a kind man—a man who sold hardware—who went and fetched it back. It was dreadfully cold in winter, but the worst was the rain. And having no watch one was afraid of being late for that train, and had to dawdle so long in the muddy streets. Of course one could look in at the pretty shops. But the little boys were so rude. Oh, no, no, not that—anything rather than be shut up in an hospital. The poor old woman did no one any harm—why shut her up?

"*Faites votre jeu, messieurs,*" cried Madame Krasinska, raking up the counters with the little rake she had had made of tortoise-shell, with a gold dragon's head for a handle—"*Rien ne va plus—vingt-trois—Rouge, impair et manque.*"

VII.

How did she come to know about this woman? She had never been inside that house over the tobacconist's, up three pairs of stairs to the left; and yet she knew exactly the pattern of the wall-paper. It was green, with a pinkish trellis-work, in the grand sitting-room, the one which was opened only on Sunday evenings, when the friends used to drop in and discuss the news, and have a game of *tresette*. You passed through the dining-room to get through it. The dining-room had no window, and was lit from a skylight; there was always a little smell of dinner in it, but that was appetising. The boys' rooms were to the back. There was a plaster Joan of Arc in the hall, close to the clothes-peg. She was painted to look like silver, and one of the boys had broken her arm, so that it looked like a gas-pipe. It was Momino who had done it, jumping on to the table when they were playing. Momino was always the scapegrace; he wore out so many pairs of trousers at the knees, but he was so warm-hearted! and after all, he had got all the prizes at school, and they all said he would be a first-rate engineer. Those dear boys! They never cost their mother a farthing, once they were sixteen; and Momino bought her a big, beautiful muff out of his own earnings as a pupil-teacher. Here it is! Such a comfort in the cold weather, you can't think, especially when gloves are too dear. Yes, it is rabbit-skin, but it is made to look like ermine, quite a handsome article. Assunta, the maid of all work, never would clean out that kitchen of hers—servants are such sluts! and she tore the moreen sofa-cover, too, against a nail in the wall. She ought to have seen that nail! But one mustn't be too hard on a poor creature, who is an orphan into the bargain. Oh, God! oh, God! and they lie in the big trench at San Martino, without even a cross over them, or a bit of wood with their name. But the white coats of the Austrians were soaked red, I warrant you! And the new dye they call magenta is made of pipe-clay—the pipe-clay the dogs clean their white coats with—and the blood of Austrians. It's a grand dye, I tell you!

Lord, Lord, how wet the poor old woman's feet are! And no fire to warm them by. The best is to go to bed when one can't dry one's clothes; and it saves lamp-oil. That was very good oil the parish priest made her a present of ... Aï, aï, how one's bones ache on the mere boards, even with a blanket over them! That good, good mattress at the pawn-shop! It's nonsense about the Italians having been beaten. The Austrians were beaten into bits, made cats'-meat of; and the volunteers are returning to-morrow. Temistocle and Momino—Momino is Girolamo, you know—will be back to-morrow; their rooms have been cleaned, and they shall have a flask of real Montepulciano.... The big bottles in the chemist's window are very beautiful, particularly the green one. The shop where they sell gloves and scarfs is also very pretty; but the English chemist's is the prettiest, because of those bottles. But they say the contents of them is all rubbish, and no real medicine.... Don't speak of San Bonifazio! I have seen it. It is where they keep the mad folk and the wretched, dirty, wicked, wicked old women.... There was a handsome book bound in red, with gold edges, on the best sitting-room table; the Æneid, translated by Caro. It was one of Temistocle's prizes. And that Berlin-wool cushion ... yes, the little dog with the cherries looked quite real....

"I have been thinking I should like to go to Sicily, to see Etna, and Palermo, and all those places," said Madame Krasinska, leaning on the balcony by the side of Prince Mongibello, smoking her fifth or sixth cigarette.

She could see the hateful hooked nose, like a nasty hawk's beak, over the big black beard, and the creature's leering, languishing black eyes, as he looked up into the twilight. She knew quite well what sort of man Mongibello was. No woman could approach him, or allow him to approach her; and there she was on that balcony alone with him in the dark, far from the rest of the party, who were dancing and talking within. And to talk of Sicily to him, who was a Sicilian too! But that was what she wanted—a scandal, a horror, anything that might deaden those thoughts which would go on inside her.... The thought of that strange, lofty whitewashed place, which she had never seen, but which she knew so well, with an altar in the middle, and rows and rows of beds, each with its set-out of bottles and baskets, and horrid slobbering and gibbering old women. Oh ... she could hear them!

"I should like to go to Sicily," she said in a tone that was now common to her, adding slowly and with emphasis, "but I should like to have someone to show me all the sights...."

"Countess," and the black beard of the creature bent over her—close to her neck—"how strange—I also feel a great longing to see Sicily once more, but not alone—those lovely, lonely valleys...."

Ah!—there was one of the creatures who had sat up in her bed and was singing, singing "Casta Diva!" "No, not alone"—she went on hurriedly, a sort of fury of satisfaction, of the satisfaction of destroying something, destroying her own fame, her own life, filling her as she felt the man's hand on her arm—"not alone, Prince—with someone to explain things—someone who knows all about it—and in this lovely spring weather. You see, I am a bad traveller—and I am afraid ... of being alone...." The last words came out of her throat loud, hoarse, and yet cracked and shrill—and just as the Prince's arm was going to clasp her, she rushed wildly into the room, exclaiming—

"Ah, I am she—I am she—I am mad!"

For in that sudden voice, so different from her own, Madame Krasinska had recognised the voice that should have issued from the cardboard mask she had once worn, the voice of Sora Lena.

VIII.

Yes, Cecchino certainly recognised her now. Strolling about in that damp May twilight among the old, tortuous streets, he had mechanically watched the big black horses draw up at the posts which closed that labyrinth of black, narrow alleys; the servant in his white waterproof opened the door, and the tall, slender woman got out and walked quickly along. And mechanically, in his wool-gathering way, he had followed the lady, enjoying the charming note of delicate pink and grey which her little frock made against those black houses, and under that wet, grey sky, streaked pink with the sunset. She walked quickly along, quite alone, having left the footman with the carriage at the entrance of that condemned old heart of Florence; and she took no notice of the stares and words of the boys playing in the gutters, the pedlars housing their barrows under the black archways, and the women leaning out of window. Yes; there was no doubt. It had struck him suddenly as he watched her pass under a double arch and into a kind of large court, not unlike that of a castle, between the frowning tall houses of the old Jews' quarter; houses escutcheoned and stanchioned, once the abode of Ghibelline nobles, now given over to rag-pickers, scavengers and unspeakable trades.

As soon as he recognised her he stopped, and was about to turn: what business has a man following a lady, prying into her doings when she goes out at twilight, with carriage and footman left several streets back, quite alone through unlikely streets? And Cecchino, who by this time was on the point of returning to the Maremma, and had come to the conclusion that civilisation was a boring and loathsome thing, reflected upon the errands which French novels described ladies as performing, when they left their carriage and footman round the corner.... But the thought was disgraceful to Cecchino, and unjust to this lady—no, no! And at this moment he stopped, for the lady had stopped a few paces before him, and was staring fixedly into the grey evening sky. There was something strange in that stare; it was not that of a woman who is hiding disgraceful proceedings. And in staring round she must have seen him; yet she stood still, like one wrapped in wild thoughts. Then suddenly she passed under the next archway, and disappeared in the dark passage of a house. Somehow Cecco Bandini could not make up his mind, as he ought to have done long ago, to turn back. He slowly passed through the oozy, ill-smelling archway, and stood before that house. It was very tall, narrow, and black as ink, with a jagged roof against the wet, pinkish sky. From the iron hook, made to hold brocades and Persian carpets on gala days of old, fluttered some rags, obscene and ill-omened in the wind. Many of the window panes were broken. It was evidently one of the houses which the municipality had condemned to destruction for sanitary reasons, and whence the inmates were gradually being evicted.

"That's a house they're going to pull down, isn't it?" he inquired in a casual tone of the man at the corner, who kept a sort of cookshop, where chestnut pudding and boiled beans steamed on a brazier in a den. Then his eye caught a half-effaced name close to the lamp-post, "Little Street of the Grave-digger." "Ah," he added quickly, "this is the street where old Sora Lena committed suicide—and—is—is that the house?"

Then, trying to extricate some reasonable idea out of the extraordinary tangle of absurdities which had all of a sudden filled his mind, he fumbled in his pocket for a silver coin, and said hurriedly to the man with the cooking brazier,

"See here, that house, I'm sure, isn't well inhabited. That lady has gone there for a charity—but—but one doesn't know that she mayn't be annoyed in there. Here's fifty centimes for your trouble. If that lady doesn't come out again in three-quarters of an hour—there! it's striking seven—just you go round to the stone posts—you'll find her carriage there—black horses and grey liveries—and tell the footman to run upstairs to his mistress—understand?" And Cecchino Bandini fled, overwhelmed at the thought of the indiscretion he was committing, but seeing, as he turned round, those rags waving an ominous salute from the black, gaunt house with its irregular roof against the wet, twilight sky.

IX.

Madame Krasinska hurried though the long black corridor, with its slippery bricks and typhoid smell, and went slowly but resolutely up the black staircase. Its steps, constructed perhaps in the days of Dante's grandfather, when a horn buckle and leathern belt formed the only ornaments of Florentine dames, were extraordinarily high, and worn off at the edges by innumerable generations of successive nobles and paupers. And as it twisted sharply on itself, the staircase was lighted at rare intervals by barred windows, overlooking alternately the black square outside, with its jags of overhanging roof, and a black yard, where a broken well was surrounded by a heap of half-sorted chickens' feathers and unpicked rags. On the first landing was an open door, partly screened by a line of drying tattered clothes; and whence issued shrill sounds of altercation and snatches of tipsy song. Madame Krasinska passed on heedless of it all, the front of her delicate frock brushing the unseen filth of those black steps, in whose crypt-like cold and gloom there was an ever-growing breath of charnel. Higher and higher, flight after flight, steps and steps. Nor did she look to the right or to the left, nor ever stop to take breath, but climbed upward, slowly, steadily. At length she reached the topmost landing, on to which fell a flickering beam of the setting sun. It issued from a room, whose door was standing wide open. Madame Krasinska entered. The room was completely empty, and comparatively light. There was no furniture in it, except a chair, pushed into a dark corner, and an empty bird-cage at the window. The panes were broken, and here and there had been mended with paper. Paper also hung, in blackened rags, upon the walls.

Madame Krasinska walked to the window and looked out over the neighbouring roofs, to where the bell in an old black belfry swung tolling the Ave Maria. There was a porticoed gallery on the top of a house some way off; it had a few plants growing in pipkins, and a drying line. She knew it all so well.

On the window-sill was a cracked basin, in which stood a dead basil plant, dry, grey. She looked at it some time, moving the hardened earth with her fingers. Then she turned to the empty bird-cage. Poor solitary starling! how he had whistled to the poor old woman! Then she began to cry.

But after a few moments she roused herself. Mechanically, she went to the door and closed it carefully. Then she went straight to the dark corner, where she knew that the staved-in straw chair stood. She dragged it into the middle of the room, where the hook was in the big rafter. She stood on the chair, and measured the height of the ceiling. It was so low that she could graze it with the palm of her hand. She took off her gloves, and then her bonnet—it was in the way of the hook. Then she unclasped her girdle, one of those narrow Russian ribbons of silver woven stuff, studded with niello. She buckled one end firmly to the big hook. Then she unwound the strip of muslin from under her collar. She was standing on the broken chair, just under the rafter. "Pater noster qui es in cælis," she mumbled, as she still childishly did when putting her head on the pillow every night.

The door creaked and opened slowly. The big, hulking woman, with the vague, red face and blear stare, and the rabbit-skin muff, bobbing on her huge crinolined skirts, shambled slowly into the room. It was the Sora Lena.

X.

When the man from the cook-shop under the archway and the footman entered the room, it was pitch dark. Madame Krasinska was lying in the middle of the floor, by the side of an overturned chair, and under a hook in the rafter whence hung her Russian girdle. When she awoke from her swoon, she looked slowly round the room; then rose, fastened her collar and murmured, crossing herself, "O God, thy mercy is infinite." The men said that she smiled.

Such is the legend of Madame Krasinska, known as Mother Antoinette Marie among the Little Sisters of the Poor.